Table of Contents

Wild Roses Ripple Lapghan, *page 57*

Readers Wrap, *page 60*

Baby Cap & Blanket, *page 63*

Large Half Flowers

Skill Level

 **INTERMEDIATE**

Pattern Notes

Stitch markers are needed for this stitch pattern.

Foundation chain is a multiple of 12 stitches plus 11; body of stitch pattern is a multiple of 11 stitches plus 9.

Work all single crochets loosely.

Chain-2 at beginning of row counts as first double crochet unless otherwise stated.

Special Stitches

Flower: Ch 5, holding yarn to left of hook, sl st from front in marked st, remove marker, ch 5, sl st in 5th ch from hook, [ch 6, sl st in 5th ch from hook] 6 times *(7-picot strand made)*, ch 5, place marker in 4th ch from hook, do not turn, rotate strand to work in underside of picots, *sk next picot, yo twice, insert hook in next unworked ch, yo, pull up lp, [yo, draw through 2 lps] twice*, rep between * 5 times, sk (last picot, sl st and next 3 chs), insert hook in next ch of ch-5 *(1 ch and 7 lps on hook)*, yo, draw through all sts on hook, ch 1.

Petal: Ch 2, dc in 2nd ch from hook.

Extended dc (ext dc): Yo, insert hook in indicated st, yo, pull up lp, yo, draw through 1 lp on hook, [yo, draw through 2 lps on hook] twice.

Cluster (cl): Keeping last lp of each st on hook, **ext dc** *(see Special Stitches)* in next dc, sk next dc, dc in next dc, sk next dc, ext dc in next st, yo, draw through all 4 lps on hook.

Large Half Flowers

Ch a multiple of 12 sts + 11 *(see Pattern Notes)* loosely, place marker in first ch from hook.

Row 1 (bottom border): Sc loosely in 2nd ch from hook and in next ch, place marker in last sc made, sc in each of next 3 chs, *work **flower** (see Special Stitches), sk next ch, sc in each of next 2 chs, holding yarn to left of hook, sl st from front in marked ch of last flower made, remove marker, sk next ch, sc in each of next 5 chs, place marker in last sc made, sc in each of next 3 chs, rep from * across to last 5 chs, sk next ch, sc in each of next 3 chs, sl st as in **front lp** (see Stitch Guide) of marked ch of last flower made, remove marker, sl st in last ch, do not turn.

Row 2: Rotate work to continue along opposite side of foundation ch, sl st in top lp of same ch as last sl st, **ch 2** *(see Pattern Notes)*, place marker in 2nd ch from hook, dc in each of next 3 chs, [**dc dec** *(see Stitch Guide)* in next 2 sts** , dc in each of next 10 sts] across, ending final rep at ** , dc in each of next 4 sts, turn.

Row 3 (start side borders): Work flower, dc in each of first 2 dc, *work **petal** (see Special Stitches), work **cl** (see Special Stitches), work petal, dc in each of next 6 sts, rep from * across, ending last rep with dc in last 2 dc, turn.

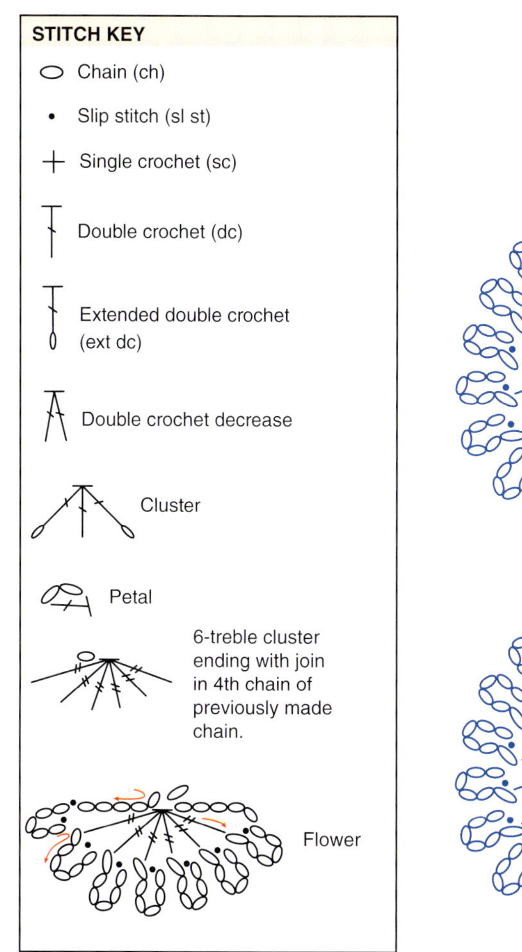

Large Half Flowers
Stitch Diagram
Note: *Reps shown in gray.*

Row 4: Work flower, dc in each of first 2 dc, *sk next petal, (**ext dc**—*see Special Stitches*, ch 1, dc, ch 1, ext dc) in next cl, sk next petal, dc in each of next 6 dc, rep from * across, ending last rep with dc in each of last 2 sts, sl st in marked ch of next flower, remove marker, turn.

Row 5: Ch 2, sk first sl st and dc, dc in next st and in each dc and ch sp across, sl st in marked ch of next flower, remove marker, turn.

Row 6: Ch 2, sk first sl st and dc, dc in each of next 7 dc, *work (petal, cl, petal, dc) in each of next 6 sts, rep from * across, ending last rep with dc in each of last 7 dc, turn.

Row 7: Ch 3 *(counts as first dc)*, place marker in 2nd ch from hook, sk first dc, dc in each of next 6 dc, *sk next petal, (ext dc, ch 1, dc, ch 1, ext dc) in next cl, sk next petal, dc in each of next 6 dc, rep from * across, ending last rep with dc in each of last 8 dc, turn.

Row 8: Ch 3 *(counts as first dc)*, place marker in 2nd ch from hook, sk first dc, dc in each dc and ch sp across, turn.

Rep rows 3–8 to desired length, ending with a row 5, excluding top border.

Top Border

Note: *See rows numbered in red on Stitch Diagram for Top Border rows.*

Row 1: Ch 1, place marker in ch just made, sk first sl st and dc, sc in next st and in each dc across to next turning ch, work **sc dec** *(see Stitch Guide)* by inserting hook in top of turning ch and in front lp of unworked ch between worked ch and picot of next flower, turn.

Row 2: Ch 1, sc in first sc, place marker in sc just made, sc in each of next 2 sc, ch 1, sl st in next sc, *work flower**, sk next sc, sc in each of next 2 sc, holding yarn to left of hook, sl st from front in marked ch of last flower made, remove marker, sc in each of next 5 sc, place marker in last sc made, sc in each of next 3 sc, rep from * ending final rep at **, sk next sc, sc in each of next 2 sc, work **sl st dec** (see Stitch Guide) in front lp of marked ch of last flower made and in both lps of next sc, sl st in next ch of same flower, remove all markers. Fasten off. ●

Medium Half Flowers

Skill Level

INTERMEDIATE

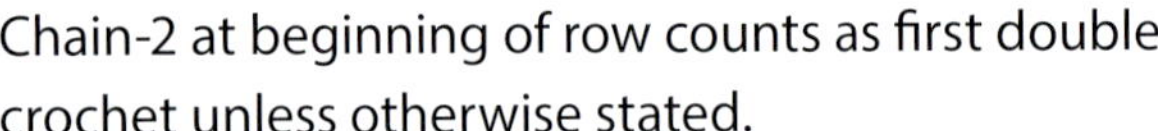

Pattern Notes

Foundation chain is a multiple of 8 chains plus 5; body of stitch pattern is a multiple of 8 stitches.

Chain-2 at beginning of row counts as first double crochet unless otherwise stated.

Chain-3 at beginning of row counts as first double crochet unless otherwise stated.

Special Stitch

Flower: Ch 5, turn, [sc in ch-4 sp, ch 4] 4 times, sc in same ch-4 sp, (5 petals made).

Medium Half Flowers

Ch a multiple of 8 sts + 5 (see Pattern Notes) loosely.

Row 1 (RS, bottom border): Sc loosely in 3rd ch from hook, [ch 4, turn, sl st in last sc made, work **flower** (see Special Stitch), sk next ch**, sc in each of next 7 chs] across, ending final rep at **, sc in last ch, do not turn.

Row 2 (start side borders): Ch 1, rotate row to work on RS along opposite side of foundation chain, sl st in first ch, ch 2, [2 dc in next st, sk next st] across, dc in **front lp** (see Stitch Guide) of first ch of first ch-2, do not turn.

Row 3: Ch 4, sl st around post of last dc made, work flower, dc in first dc, [2 dc in next dc, sk next dc] across to last 2 sts, ch 2, (sl st, ch 4, sl st) in top of ch-2, work flower, do not turn.

Row 4: Sl st in top of next ch-2, **ch 2** (see Pattern Notes), [2 dc in next dc, sk next dc] across to last 2 sts, sk next dc, dc in last dc, turn.

Row 5: Ch 3 (see Pattern Notes), [2 dc in next dc, sk next dc] across to last 2 sts, dc in top of ch-2, turn.

Row 6: Ch 3, [2 dc in next dc, sk next dc] across, dc in top of last st, do not turn.

Rep rows 3–6 for pattern, ending with a row 6 at desired length excluding border.

Top Border

Note: *See rows numbered in red on Stitch Diagram for Top Border rows.*

Row 1: Rep row 3, ending with ch-1 after working last flower.

Row 2: Sk ch-2, sc in each dc across, turn.

Row 3: Ch 1, sc in next sc, [ch 4, turn, sl st in last sc made, work flower, sk next sc**, sc in next 7 sc] across, ending final rep at **, sc in next st, sl st in last sc. Fasten off. ●

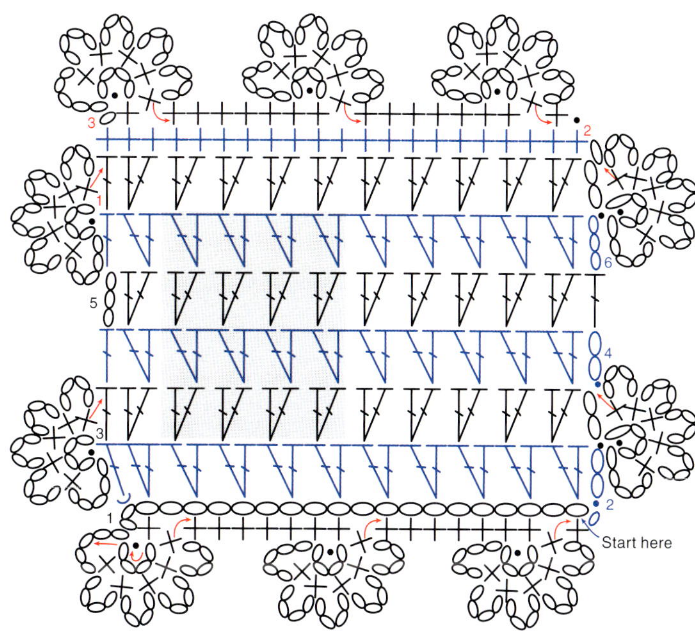

Medium Half Flowers
Stitch Diagram
Note: *Reps shown in gray.*

STITCH KEY

◯ Chain (ch)

• Slip stitch (sl st)

⌣ Front loop

+ Single crochet (sc)

T Double crochet (dc)

Puff Blossoms

Skill Level

■■■□ **INTERMEDIATE**

Pattern Note

Foundation chain is a multiple of 8 stitches plus 5; body of stitch pattern between side borders is a multiple of 5 stitches plus 4.

Special Stitches

Small puff: [Yo, insert hook, pull up long lp] twice in indicated st, yo, draw through all 5 lps on hook.

Large puff: [Yo, insert hook, pull up long lp] 3 times in indicated st, yo, draw through all 7 lps on hook.

Flower top: Work ([**large puff** *(see Special Stitches)*, ch 2] twice, large puff) in next flower eyelet.

Flower bottom: [Yo, insert hook, pull up lp] twice in 4th ch from hook, sk hdc, [yo, insert hook, pull up lp] 3 times in next ch, sk (sl st, ch sp, sl st), [yo, insert hook, pull up lp] 3 times in next ch, yo, pull through all 17 lps on hook, ch 4, **small puff** *(see Special Stitches)* in eyelet at base of ch-4 *(4 petals made)*.

Picot: Ch 1, sl st in last st made.

Puff Blossoms

Ch a multiple of 8 sts + 5 *(see Pattern Note)*.

Row 1 (start bottom border): [Yo, insert hook, pull up lp] twice in 3rd ch from hook, sk 3 chs, [yo, insert hook, pull up lp] 3 times in next ch, sk 3 chs, [yo, insert hook, pull up lp] 3 times in next ch, yo, pull through all 17 lps on hook, ch 4, **small puff** *(see Special Stitches)* in eyelet at base of ch-4, *ch 4, [yo, insert hook, pull up lp] twice in 4th ch from hook, sk 3 chs, [yo, insert hook, pull up lp] 3 times in next ch, sk 3 chs, [yo, insert hook, pull up lp] 3 times in next ch, yo, pull through all 17 lps on hook, ch 4**, small puff in eyelet at base of ch-4, rep from * across,

ending final rep at **, [yo, insert hook, pull up lp] twice in 4th ch from hook, yo, insert hook in last ch, yo, pull up lp, yo, pull through 2 lps, yo, pull through rem lps on hook, turn.

Row 2: Ch 3, [work **flower top** *(see Special Stitches)***, ch 1] across, ending final rep at **, sk next petal, dc in next ch-3 sp, turn.

Row 3: Ch 4, sl st in next ch-2 sp, [ch 2, sl st in next ch-2 sp, ch 4, sk next ch-1 sp, sl st in next ch-2 sp] across, ending last rep with sl st in last ch-2 sp, ch 1, hdc in last ch-3 sp, turn.

Row 4 (start side borders): Ch 6, work **flower bottom** *(see Special Stitches)*, ch 1, sk next 3 chs, [dc in next sl st, 2 dc in next ch-2 sp, dc in next sl st], *ch 5, work flower bottom**, sk next 3 chs, rep between [ ], rep from * across, ending final rep at **, dc in last ch sp, turn.

Row 5: Ch 3, work flower top, ch 1, sk next ch sp, *dc in each of next 4 dc, ch 1, work flower top**, sk next ch sp, rep from * across, ending final rep at **, dc in last ch sp, turn.

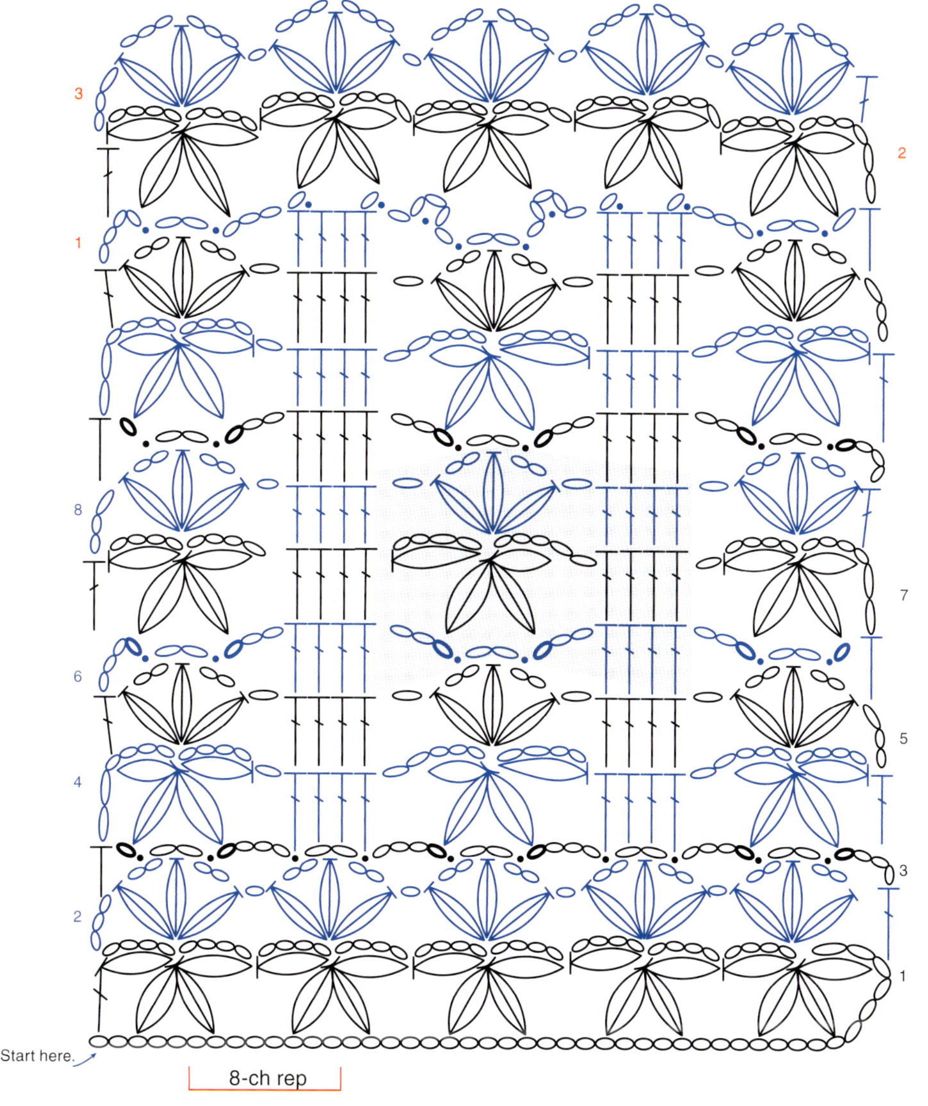

Puff Blossoms
Stitch Diagram
Note: *Reps shown in gray.*

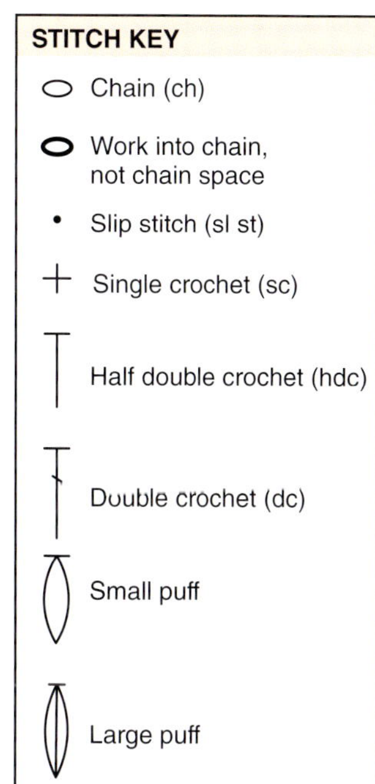

Row 6: Ch 4, sl st in next ch-2 sp, ch 2, sl st in next ch-2 sp, ch 3, sk next ch-1 sp, *dc in each of next 4 dc, ch 3, sk (ch-2 sp, large puff), sl st in next ch-2 sp, ch 2, sl st in next ch-2 sp**, ch 3, rep from * across, ending final rep at **, ch 1, hdc in top of turning ch, turn.

Row 7: Ch 6, work flower bottom, ch 1, sk next ch sp, dc in each of next 4 dc, *ch 5, work flower bottom**, dc in each of next 4 dc, rep from * across, ending final rep at **, dc in last ch sp, turn.

Row 8: Ch 3, work flower top, ch 1, sk next ch sp, dc in each of next 4 dc, *ch 1, work flower top**, ch 1, dc in each of next 4 dc, rep from * across, ending final rep at **, dc in last ch sp, turn.

Rep rows 6–8 to desired length minus the length of the bottom border.

Top Border

Note: *See rows numbered in red on Stitch Diagram for Top Border rows.*

Row 1: Ch 4, sl st in next ch-2 sp, ch 2, sl st in next ch-2 sp, ch 3, sk next ch-1 sp, dc in next dc, work **picot** *(see Special Stitches)*, dc in each of next 3 sts, work picot, *ch 4, sl st in 3rd ch from hook, ch 1, sl st in next ch-2 sp, ch 2, sl st in next ch-2 sp**, ch 4, sl st in 3rd ch from hook, dc in next st, work picot, dc in each of next 3 sts, work picot, rep from * across, ending final rep at **, ch 1, hdc in turning ch.

Row 2: Ch 6, work flower bottom, *ch 4, starting 2nd puff in next picot and 3rd puff in next picot, work flower bottom, rep from * through last picot, ch 4, work flower bottom to point where you have pulled a yo through 17 lps on hook, [yo, insert hook, pull up lp] twice in 4th ch from hook, yo, insert hook in last ch sp, yo, pull up lp, yo, pull through 2 lps, yo, pull through rem lps on hook, turn.

Row 3: Ch 3, *([large puff, ch 3] twice, large puff) in next flower center**, ch 1, rep from * across, ending final rep at **, dc in last ch sp. Fasten off. ●

Twisted Loops

Skill Level

■■■■□ INTERMEDIATE

Pattern Notes

Stitch markers are needed for this stitch pattern.

Foundation chain is a multiple of 3 stitches plus 2; body of stitch pattern between side borders is a multiple of 3 stitches plus 2.

Chain-3 at beginning of row counts as first double crochet unless otherwise stated.

Rows with side borders contain extra short-row turns.

Special Stitches

Reverse slip stitch (rev sl st): Sl st from back to front in indicated lp or st.

Twisted loop: Ch 5, with yarn held to right of hook, **rev sl st** *(see Special Stitches)* in indicated lp of indicated st. Keep all twisted loops on RS of work.

Right side double crochet (RS dc) and right side single crochet (RS sc): When working a dc or sc into a st from the RS that already has a twisted lp slip stitched into either the front or back lp, insert the hook under both lps to the left of the sl st, but in the same st.

Twisted Loops

Ch a multiple of 3 sts + 2 *(see Pattern Notes)* loosely.

Row 1 (WS, start bottom border): Working loosely in **back lps only** *(see Stitch Guide)*, sc in 2nd ch from hook and in each ch across, turn.

Row 2: Sl st in first st, mark front lp of st just made, [sk next 2 sts, work **twisted loop** *(see Special Stitches)* in front lp of next st] across, mark back lp of last sl st made, turn.

Row 3: Working in front of twisted loops in same row as sl sts just made, sk first worked st and next unworked st, [work twisted loop in back lp of next unworked st, sk next worked and next unworked st] across, ending after last rep with twisted loop in last unworked st, sl st normally in marked lp of last sl st, remove marker, turn.

Row 4 (RS): Ch 3 *(see Pattern Notes)*, working behind twisted loops and into sts from row 1, sk st at base of ch-3, dc in each of next 2 sts, ***RS dc** *(see Special Stitches)* in each of next 2 sts, dc in next st, rep from * across ending with 1 dc in marked st from row 2, turn.

Row 5: Ch 3, dc in each dc across, turn.

Rows 6–13: [Rep rows 2–5] twice.

Row 14 (RS, start side borders):

A. Sl st in both lps of first st, mark front lp of sl st just made, [sk next 2 sts, work twisted loop in front lp of next st] 3 times, mark back lp of last sl st made, turn;

B. working with twisted loops folded out of the way and in same row as sl sts just made, sk first occupied st and next unworked st, [work twisted loop in back lp of next unworked st, sk next occupied and next unworked st] twice, work twisted loop in last unworked st, sl st normally in marked lp of last sl st, turn;

C. ch 3, working in row below and moving loops away, dc in each of next 2 sts, [RS dc in each of next 2 sts, dc in next st] twice, sc in back lp of next st, dc in each st across to last 10 sts, ch 3, sl st in next dc, mark front lp of sl st just made, [sk next 2 sts, work twisted loop in front lp of next st] 3 times, mark back lp of last sl st made, turn;

D. working with twisted loops folded out of the way and in same row as sl sts just made, [sk next occupied st and next unworked st, work twisted loop in back lp of next unworked st] twice, sk next occupied and next unworked st, ch 5, sl st normally in marked lp of last sl st, turn;

E. ch 2, sk first dc and the sl st in it, dc in next st, [dc in next unworked dc, work RS dc in each of next 2 dc] twice, dc in last unworked st, dc in marked lp of next sl st, remove all markers, turn.

Row 15 (WS): Ch 3, dc in each of next 8 dc, **dc dec** *(see Stitch Guide)* with first step in same st as last dc made and 2nd step in next ch-3 sp, dc in each st across, turn.

Rep rows 14 and 15 until desired length is achieved minus length of bottom border.

Next 10 rows (start top border): [Rep rows 2–5 consecutively] 3 times, ending with a row 3.

Last row: Ch 1, working in same row as twisted loops, work sc in next st, [sc in next unworked st, work RS sc in each of next 2 sts] across to last 2 sts, sc in next unworked st, sk last worked st of same row, sl st in back lp of marked sl st, remove marker. Fasten off. ●

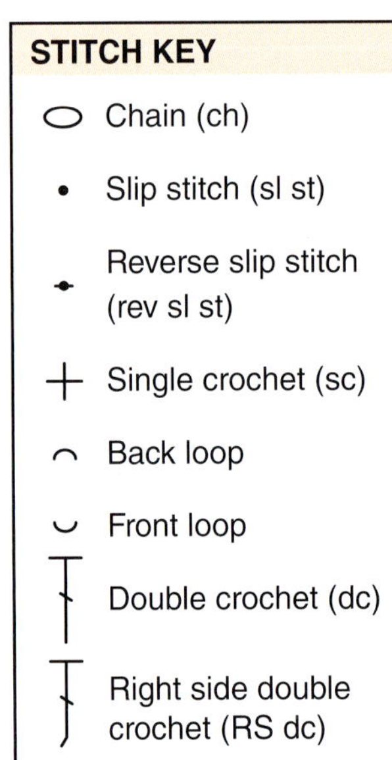

STITCH KEY

◯ Chain (ch)

• Slip stitch (sl st)

◆ Reverse slip stitch (rev sl st)

+ Single crochet (sc)

⌒ Back loop

⌣ Front loop

Double crochet (dc)

Right side double crochet (RS dc)

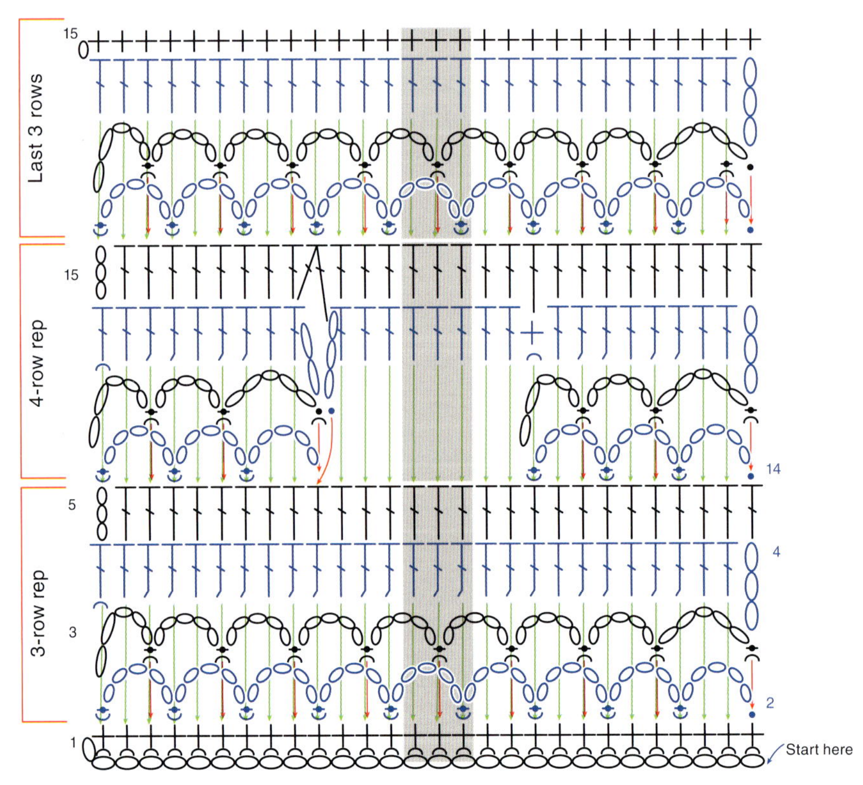

Twisted Loops
Stitch Diagram
Note: *Reps shown in gray.*

Zigzag Popcorns

Skill Level

 INTERMEDIATE

Pattern Notes

Foundation chain is a multiple of 4 stitches plus 1; body of stitch pattern between side borders is a multiple of 4 stitches plus 2.

Lower part of last double crochet of row 1 should be folded to wrong side of work when weaving in yarn end; yarn end from fasten off should secure last stitch to last side stitch.

Special Stitches

Popcorn (pc): Work 5 dc in designated st, remove hook from working lp and insert it in top of first dc made from back to front on WS or from front to back on RS, insert hook in working lp and draw through.

Beginning popcorn (beg pc): Work 5 dc in designated st, remove hook from working lp and insert it in top ch of turning ch from back to front on WS or from front to back on RS, insert hook in working lp and draw through.

Picot: Ch 3, sl st from front to back to front around post of last dc worked, do not sk next dc.

Zigzag Popcorns

Ch a multiple of 4 sts + 1 *(see Pattern Notes).*

Row 1 (WS, start bottom border): Sl st in back lp only of 2nd ch from hook, ch 2, working in both lps of ch, 5 dc in next ch, remove hook from lp, insert hook from back to front in top of 2nd dc made and in dropped lp, draw lp through, [ch 1, sk next ch, dc in each of next 2 chs, work **pc** *(see Special Stitches)* in next ch] across to last 2 chs, ch 1, 2 dc in last ch, turn.

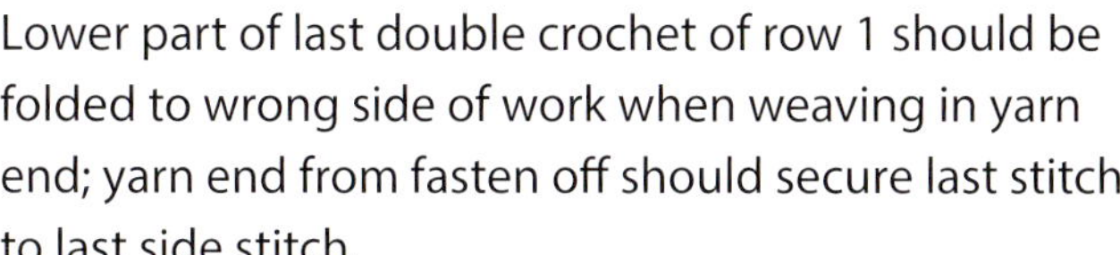

Row 2 (RS): Ch 3, work pc in first dc, ch 1, sk next 2 sts, [dc in next pc, work pc in next dc, ch 1, sk next dc, dc in next ch sp] across, sk last pc, work pc in next dc, ch 1, dc in top ch of turning ch, turn.

Row 3 (start side borders): Ch 3, sk first 2 sts, work **beg pc** *(see Special Stitches)* in next pc, ch 1, sk next dc, [dc in next ch sp, dc in next pc**, work **picot** *(see Special Stitches)*, dc in each of next 2 dc, work picot] across, ending last rep at ** in next-to-last pc, dc in next dc, sk next ch sp and pc, work pc in top ch of turning ch, turn.

Row 4: Ch 3, work beg pc in first pc, ch 1, sk next dc, ignoring picots and folding to RS, dc in each dc across, dc in next ch sp, work pc in next pc, turn.

Row 5: Ch 3, work beg pc in first pc, ch 1, sk next dc, [dc in each of next 2 dc, work picot] across to last 4 sts, dc in each of next 2 dc, dc in next ch sp, work pc in next pc, turn.

[Rep rows 4 and 5 alternately] to desired length minus length of bottom border, ending with a row 4.

Top Border

Note: *See rows numbered in red on Stitch Diagram for Top Border rows.*

Row 1: Ch 3, work beg pc in first pc, ch 2, dc in next dc, [work pc in next dc, ch 1, sk next dc** , dc in each of next 2 dc] across, ending final rep at ** , dc in next dc, dc in next ch sp, work pc in last pc, turn.

Row 2: Ch 4, work beg pc in first pc, ch 1, sk next 2 dc, [dc in next ch sp, dc in next pc, work pc in next dc, ch 1, sk next dc] across to last ch-2 sp, leaving rem sts unworked, ch 1 and pull tight to secure. Fasten off. ●

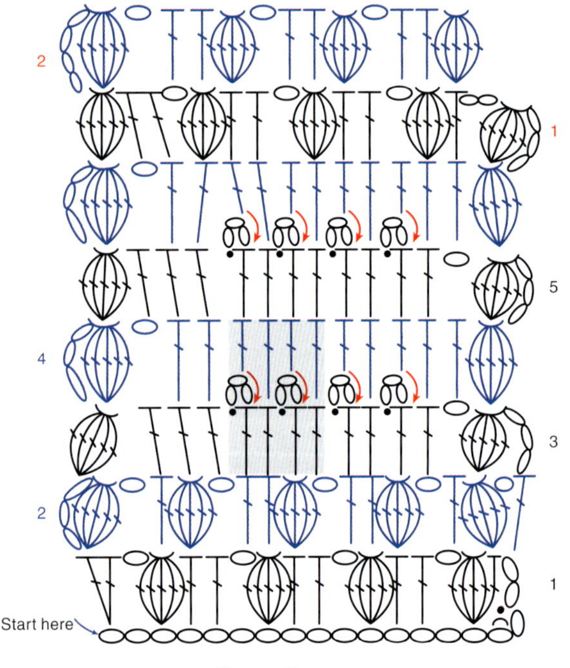

Zigzag Popcorns
Stitch Diagram
Note: *Reps shown in gray.*

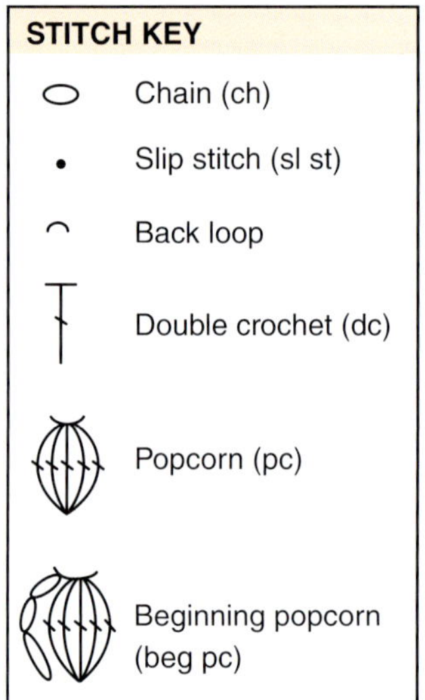

Zigzag Chain Braids

Skill Level

INTERMEDIATE

Pattern Notes

Use different-colored stitch markers to keep braided plaits organized.

Foundation chain is a multiple of 4 stitches plus 1; body of stitch pattern between borders is a multiple of 4 stitches plus 2.

Special Stitches

Plait: Ch 13, sl st in 2 lps of 13th ch from hook. Keep plaits on RS.

Fastening Stitch (FS): Insert hook in last plait pulled up, yo, pull lp through plait only, yo, insert hook in designated dc, yo, pull up lp, yo, draw through 2 lps on hook, yo, draw through all 3 lps on hook.

Extended half double crochet (ext hdc): Yo, insert hook, yo, pull up lp, yo, draw through 1 lp on hook, yo, draw through all 3 lps on hook.

Front lower bar: This is the 3rd lp or strand that is formed when a hdc is worked; to make the 2 top lps appear on the RS of the fabric, work into this 3rd lp or bar.

Zigzag Chain Braids

Ch a multiple of 4 sts + 1 *(see Pattern Notes)*.

Row 1 (WS, start bottom border): Sc loosely in 2nd ch from hook, sc in next ch, sl st in next ch, work **plait** *(see Special Stitches)*, mark plait just made as beg plait of left-side border, [sl st in next ch, sc in each of next 2 chs, sl st in next ch, work plait] across to last ch, mark last plait made as beg plait of right-side border, sl st in next ch, sc in last ch, turn.

Row 2 (RS): Ch 3, sk plaits throughout, sk first 2 sl sts, 2 dc in next sc, work plait, mark plait just made as 2nd plait of right-side border, [2 dc in next sc, sk next 2 sl sts, 2 dc in next sc, work plait] across to last sc, mark last plait made as 2nd plait of left-side border, dc in last sc, turn.

Row 3: Ch 3, sk first dc, sk plaits by working in front of them throughout, dc in each of next 2 dc, work plait, dc in each dc across to last dc, dc in last dc, work plait, dc in top of turning ch, turn.

Row 4: Ch 3, sk first dc, sk next plait, dc in each of next 2 dc, work plait, dc in next dc, ignoring marked side plaits and taking care not to twist plaits, pull next (unmarked) plait in row below through 2nd (unmarked) plait 2 rows below, [work **FS** *(see Special Stitches)* in next dc, dc in each of next 3 dc**, pull next plait in row below through next plait 2 rows below] across, ending final rep at **, dc in each of next 3 dc, sk next plait, work plait, dc in top of turning ch, turn.

Row 5: Ch 3, sk first dc, sk plaits, dc in each of next 2 dc, work plait, **ext hdc** *(see Special Stitches)* in each st across to last 2 dc, dc in each of next 2 dc, work plait, dc in top of turning ch, turn.

Row 6: Ch 3, sk first st, skipping plaits, dc in each of next 2 dc, work plait, next hdc in back lp of each st across to last 2 dc, dc in each of next 2 dc, work plait, dc in top of turning ch, turn.

Row 7: Ch 3, sk first dc, sk plaits, dc in each of next 2 dc, work plait, ext hdc in **front lower bar** *(see Special Stitches)* of each st across to last 2 dc, dc in each of next 2 dc, work plait, dc in top of turning ch, turn.

[Rep rows 6 and 7] to desired length minus length of bottom border, ending with a row 6.

Top Border

Note: See rows numbered in red on Stitch Diagram for Top Border rows.

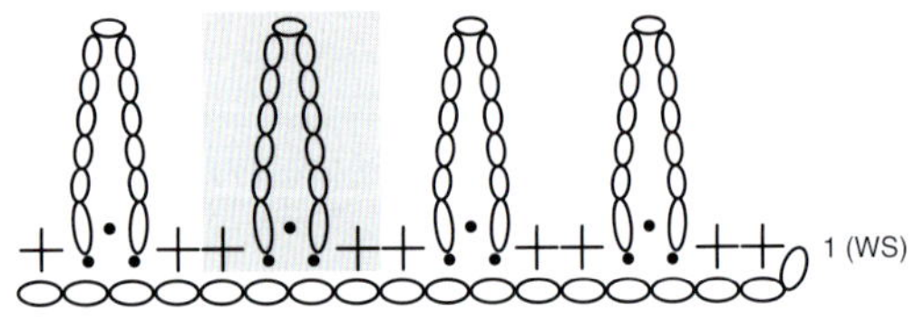

Zigzag Chain Braids
Row 1
Note: Reps shown in gray.

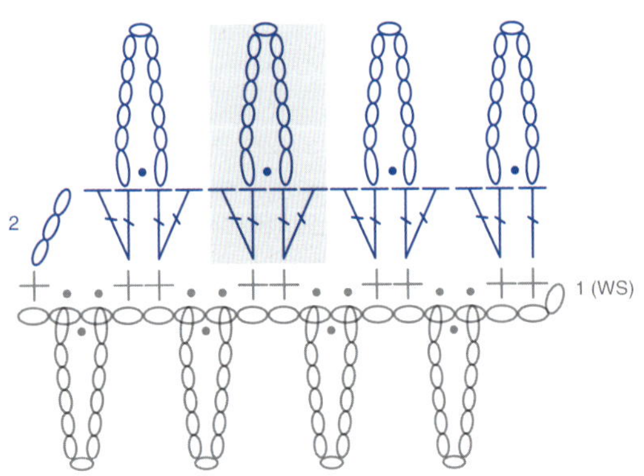

Zigzag Chain Braids
Row 2
Note: Reps shown in gray.

Row 1: Ch 3, sk first dc, skipping plaits, dc in each of next 2 dc, [work plait, ext hdc in back lp of each of next 4 sts] across, ending final rep with ext hdc in back lp of each of next 2 sts, dc in each of next 2 dc, work plait, dc in top of turning ch, turn.

Row 2: Ch 3, sk first dc, sk plaits, dc in each of next 2 dc, [work plait, dc in back lps of each of next 4 sts] across, ending final rep with dc in back lps of each of next 2 sts, dc normally in each of next 2 dc, work plait, dc in top of turning ch, turn.

Row 3: Ch 3, sk first dc, sk plaits, dc in each of next 2 dc, dc in back lps only of each dc across to last 2 dc, dc in each of next 2 dc, dc in top of turning ch, turn.

Row 4: Ch 2, working on RS, braid right-edge border plaits tog as follows: ◊Taking care not to twist plaits, working from bottom, pull marked 2nd side-border plait through marked beg side-border plait, zigzagging plaits, continue to pull each plait through the plait above it to top◊, work FS in first dc, dc in each of next 2 dc, dc in **front lp only** *(see Stitch Guide)* of next dc, [pull next plait in row below through plait 2 rows directly below, work FS in front lp only of next dc, dc in front lps only of each of next 3 dc] across to 3 dc from end, work from ◊ to ◊ to braid left-edge border plaits tog, work FS in front lp only of next dc, dc normally in each of next 2 dc, dc in top of turning ch. Fasten off. ●

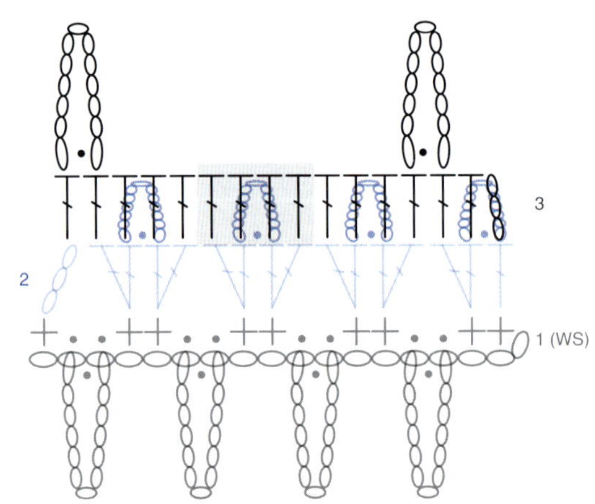

Zigzag Chain Braids
Row 3
Note: Reps shown in gray.

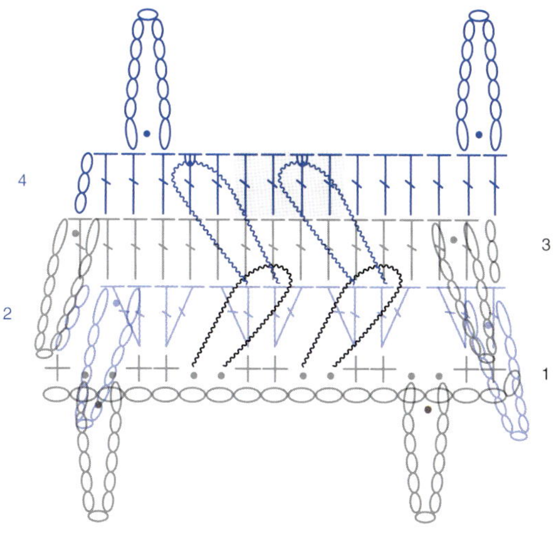

Zigzag Chain Braids
Row 4
Note: *Reps shown in gray.*

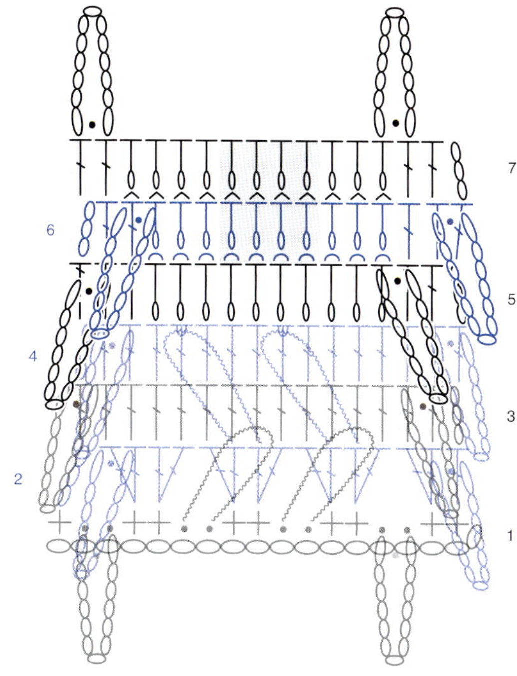

Zigzag Chain Braids
Row reps
Note: *Reps shown in gray.*

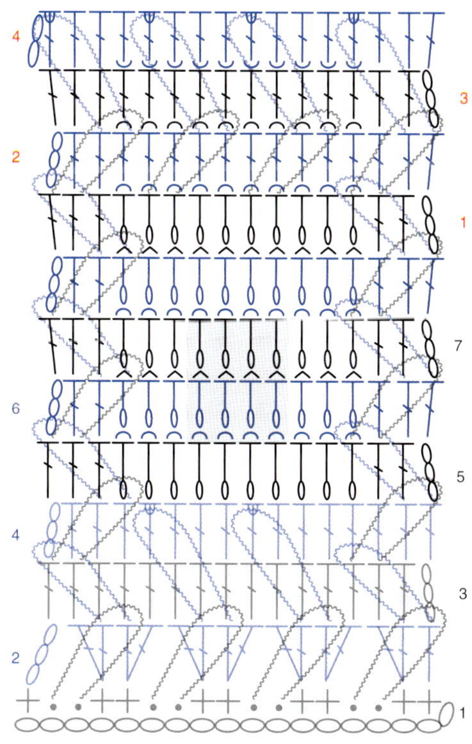

Zigzag Chain Braids
Stitch Diagram
Note: *Reps shown in gray.*

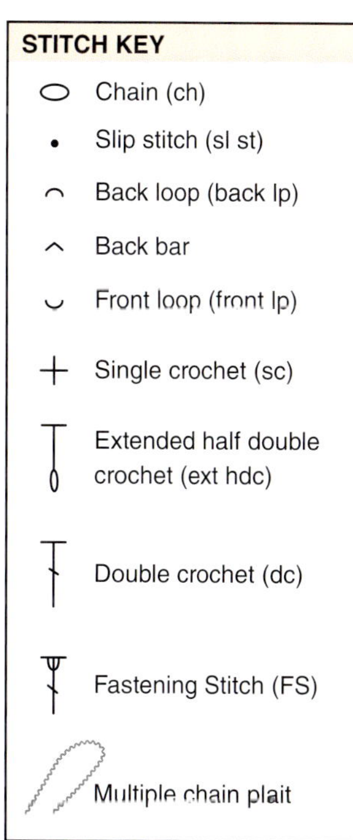

Puff Pairs

Skill Level

■■■□ **INTERMEDIATE**

Pattern Notes

Foundation chain is a multiple of 9 stitches plus 5; body of stitch pattern between side borders is a multiple of 9 stitches plus 2.

Chain-3 at beginning of row counts as first double crochet unless otherwise stated.

Special Stitches

Puff: [Yo, insert hook, pull up long lp] 4 times in indicated st, yo, and draw through all 9 lps on hook.

Puff pair: [Work **puff** *(see Special Stitches)*, ch 4, work puff] in indicated st.

Puff Pairs

Ch a multiple of 9 sts + 5 *(see Pattern Notes)*.

Bottom Border

Row 1: Dc in 5th ch from hook, *ch 2, sk 3 chs, dc in next ch, ch 2, sk 3 chs, dc in each of next 2 chs, rep from * across, turn.

Row 2: Ch 3 *(see Pattern Notes)*, dc in next dc, *ch 1, work **puff pair** *(see Special Stitches)* in next dc, ch 2, dc in each of next 2 dc, rep from * across, turn.

Row 3: Ch 3, dc in next dc, *ch 2, sc in next ch-4 sp, ch 2, dc in each of next 2 dc, rep from * across, turn.

Side Borders

Row 4: Ch 3, dc in next dc, ch 1, work puff pair in next sc, ch 2, *dc in each of next 2 dc**, [2 dc in next ch sp] twice, rep from * across, ending final rep at ** before final (ch 2, sc, ch 2), ch 1, work puff pair in last sc, ch 2, dc in each of last 2 sts, turn.

Row 5: Ch 3, dc in next dc, ch 2, sc in next ch-4 sp, ch 2, dc in each of next 2 dc, *dc in next st, work puff in next st, ch 1, sk 1 st, dc in each of next 3 sts, rep from * across to ch-2 sp, ch 2, sc in next ch-4 sp, ch 2, dc in each of last 2 sts, turn.

Row 6: Ch 3, dc in next st, ch 1, work puff pair in next sc, ch 2, dc in each of next 2 sts, *dc in each of next 4 sts**, work puff in next st, ch 1, sk 1 st, rep from * across to last 2 dc before side border, ending final rep at **, dc in each of next 2 sts, ch 1, work puff pair in next sc, ch 2, dc in each of last 2 sts, turn.

Row 7: Rep row 5.

[Rep rows 6 and 7 alternately] to desired length minus length of bottom border.

Top Border

Note: *See rows numbered in red on Stitch Diagram for Top Border rows.*

Row 1: Ch 3, dc in next st, [ch 1, work puff pair in next sc, ch 2], dc in each st across to side border, rep between [ ], dc in each of last 2 sts, turn.

"

Row 2: Ch 3, dc in next st, ch 2, sc in ch-4 sp, ch 2, dc in each of next 2 sts, *ch 2, sk 2 sts, dc in sp between last sk dc and next dc, ch 2, sk 2 dc, dc in each of next 2 dc, rep from * across to side border, ch 2, sc in ch-4 sp, ch 2, dc in each of last 2 sts, turn.

Row 3: Rep Bottom Border row 2.

Row 4: Rep Bottom Border row 3. Fasten off. ●

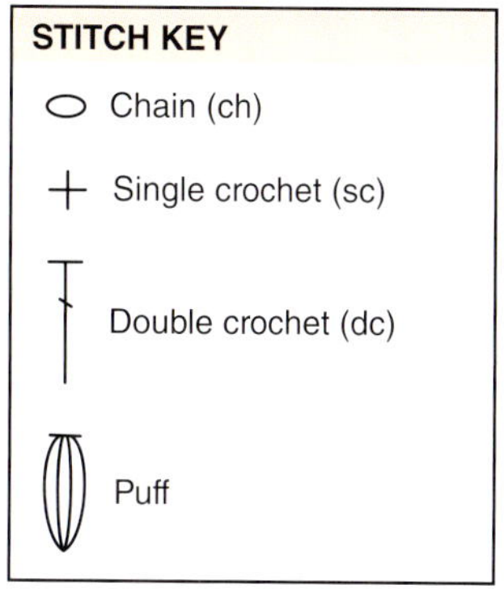

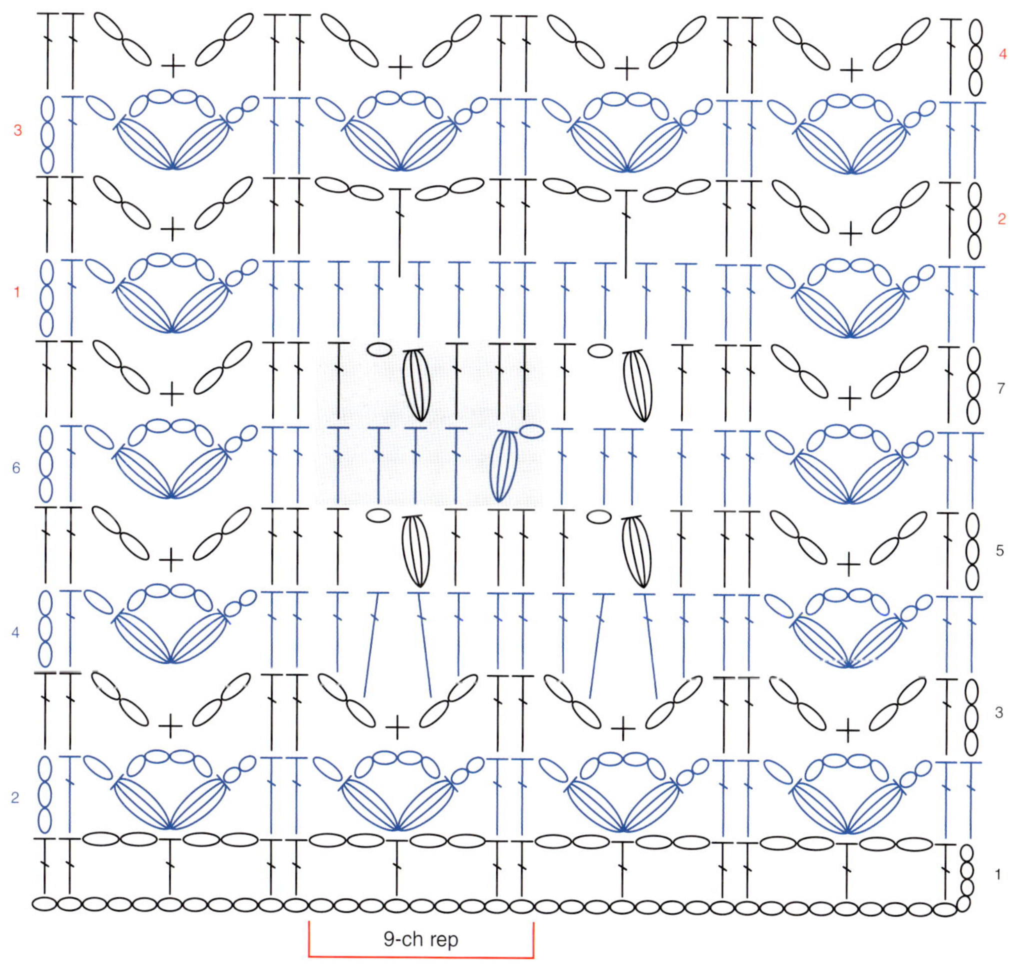

Puff Pairs
Stitch Diagram
Note: *Reps shown in gray.*

Spiral Rosettes

Skill Level

◀■■■▷ **INTERMEDIATE**

Pattern Note
Body of stitch pattern between side borders is a multiple of 4 stitches plus 3.

Special Stitches
Spiral Rosette (SR): Ch 7, with ridge lps facing away, unless instructed otherwise, working in **back lp only** *(see Stitch Guide)* of chs throughout, 2 sc in 2nd ch from hook, 3 sc in each of next 4 chs, sc in last ch.

Twisted double crochet (twisted dc): With WS facing, insert hook from back to front in last st or turning ch, yo, pull up lp, [yo, draw through 2 lps on hook] twice.

Spiral Rosettes
Row 1 (RS, bottom border): Work **SR** *(see Special Stitches)*, [ch 2, work SR] across to approximate desired width, excluding intended side borders, do not turn.

Row 2 (RS, start side borders): Ch 1, work SR, turn, taking care not to twist work, dc around next unworked ch-1, [ch 1, sk post of next sc, dc in 1 lp of next occupied ch**, ch 1, dc around next free ch-2] across, ending last rep at ** in last ch, work SR, sc in same ch st as last dc made, turn.

Row 3: Ch 4, working in front of last SR made, sl st in first dc, ch 3 *(counts as dc and ch-1)*, sk next ch sp, dc in next dc, [ch 1, dc in next dc] across to last ch sp, ch 1, sk next ch sp, work **twisted dc** *(see Special Stitches)* in last dc.

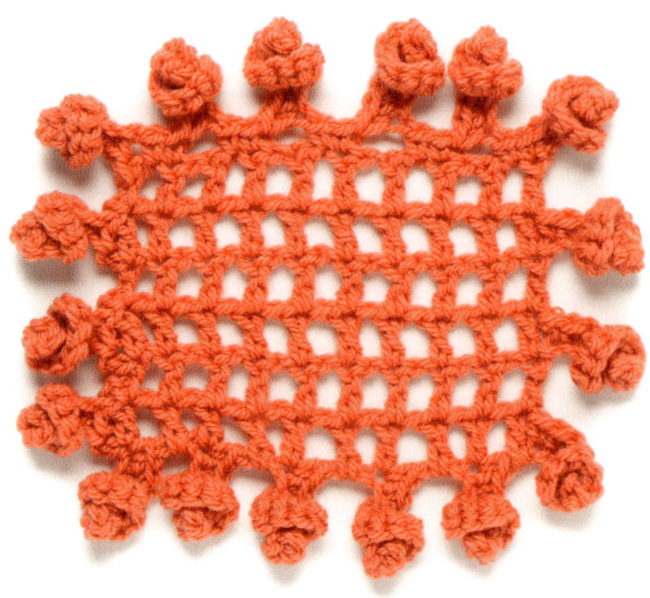

Row 4: Work SR, dc in next twisted dc, [ch 1, dc in next dc] across, work SR, sc in same ch st as last dc made, turn.

[Rep rows 3 and 4] to desired length minus length of bottom border.

Top Border
Note: *See row numbered in red on Stitch Diagram for Top Border rows.*

Row 1: Work SR, sc in next twisted dc, [sc in next ch, work SR, sk next 2 sts, sc in next dc] across to last ch sp, sc in next ch st, ch 1, work SR, sk next ch, sl st in last ch. Fasten off. ●

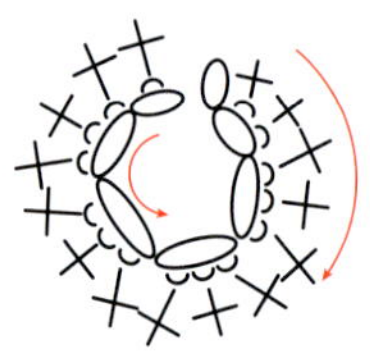

SPIRAL ROSETTE STITCH KEY

⬭	Chain (ch)
+	Single crochet (sc)
⌒	Work in back loop only
→	Work in direction of arrow

Spiral Rosettes
Spiral Rosette Stitch Diagram

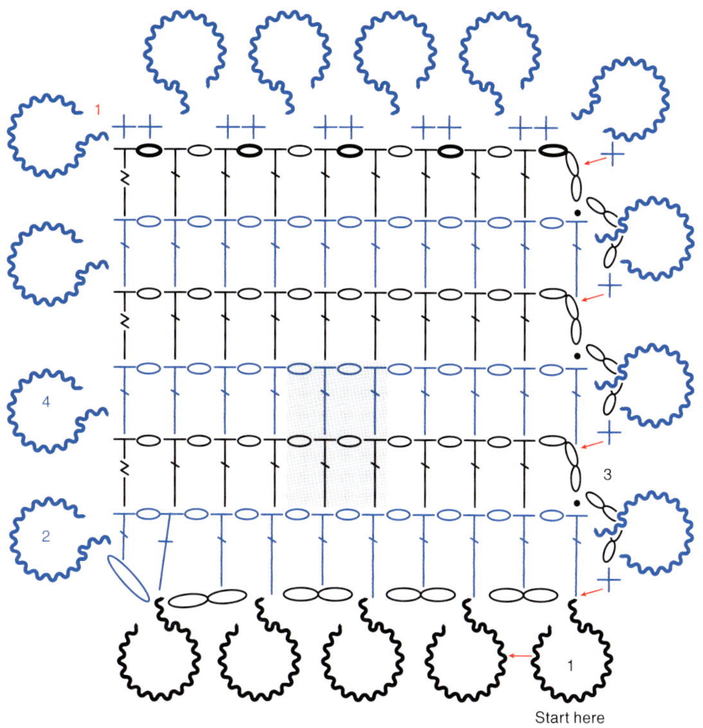

Spiral Rosettes
Stitch Diagram
Note: *Reps shown in gray.*

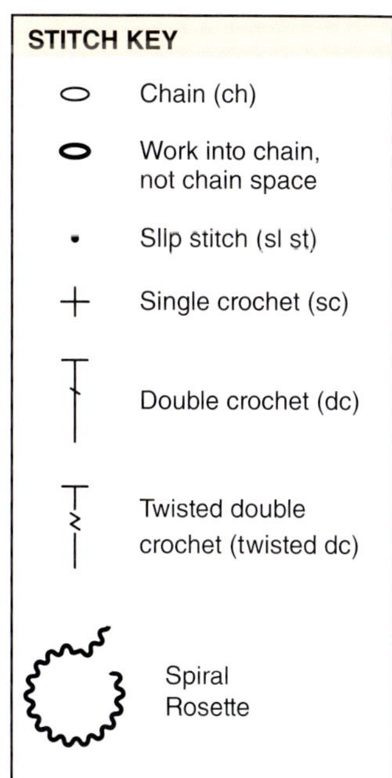

Double Crochet Shells

Skill Level

INTERMEDIATE

Pattern Note

Foundation chain is a multiple of 10 stitches plus 9; body of stitch pattern is a multiple of 6 stitches plus 5.

Special Stitches

Shell: (3 dc, ch 2, 3 dc) in indicated st.

End shell: (3 dc, ch 2, 4 hdc) in last sl st, turn, ch 1 loosely, sk 1 hdc, sl st in each of next 2 hdc, ch 1, sl st loosely in next hdc, sl st normally in ch-2 sp.

Double Crochet Shells

Ch a multiple of 10 sts + 9 *(see Pattern Note).*

Bottom Border

Row 1 (RS): Work **shell** *(see Special Stitches)* in 4th ch from hook, [taking care not to twist work, sl st around base ch, work shell in 10th ch from last shell made] across, ending last rep with (3 dc, ch 2, 3 hdc) in 6th ch from end, sl st in last ch, turn.

Row 2: Ch 1 loosely, sk first sl st, sk first hdc, sl st loosely in next hdc, ch 1, sl st loosely in next hdc, sl st normally in next ch-2 sp, [ch 9, sl st in next ch-2 sp] across, turn.

Row 3: Ch 4, [work shell in next sl st at top of shell from previous row, sl st in next ch-9 sp] across to last shell of previous row, work **end shell** *(see Special Stitches)* in next sl st.

Row 4: [Ch 9, sl st in next ch-2 sp] across, turn.

Row 5: Rep row 3.

Row 6: [Ch 9, sl st in next ch-2 sp] twice, [ch 7, sl st in next ch-2 sp] across, ending last rep in 3rd shell from end of row, [ch 9, sl st in next ch-2 sp] twice, turn.

Side Borders

Row 7: Ch 4, [work shell in next sl st, sl st in next ch-9 sp] twice, 2 dc in same ch-9 sp, [dc in next sl st, 5 dc in next ch-7 sp] across to end of last ch-7 sp, dc in next sl st, 2 dc in next ch-9 sp, sl st in same sp, work shell in next sl st, sl st in next ch-9 sp, work end shell in last sl st, turn.

Row 8: Ch 9, sl st in next ch-2 sp, ch 7, sk rem of shell and next sl st, dc in each dc across to next sl st, ch 7, sk next sl st, sl st in next ch-2 sp, ch 9, sl st in next ch-2 sp, turn.

Row 9: Ch 4, work shell in next sl st, sl st in next ch-9 sp, work shell in next sl st, sl st in next ch-7 sp, dc in each dc across to next ch-7 sp, sl st in next ch-7 sp, work shell in next sl st, sl st in next ch-9 sp, work end shell in next sl st, turn.

[Rep rows 8 and 9] to desired length minus length of Bottom Border, ending with a row 9.

Top Border

Note: *See rows numbered in red on Stitch Diagram for Top Border rows.*

Row 1: Ch 9, sl st in next shell, ch 9, sk (rem of shell, next sl st, and next 2 dc), [sc in next dc, ch 9, sk next 5 dc] across to last 2 dc in body, ch 9, sk (next 2 dc, sl st, and first half of shell), sl st in next ch-2 sp, ch 9, sl st in next ch-2 sp, turn.

Row 2: Ch 4, [shell in next sl st, sl st in next ch-9 sp] twice, [shell in next sc, sl st in next ch-9 sp] across to last 2 shells, shell in next sl st, sl st in next ch-9 sp, end shell in next sl st.

Rows 3–5: Alternately, [rep Bottom Border rows 4 and 5] twice, ending with row 4.

Row 6: Ch 4, [shell in next sl st, sl st in next ch-9 sp] across to last sl st, (dc, 2 hdc, ch 1, 3 hdc, dc) in last sl st. Fasten off. ●

STITCH KEY	
⬭	Chain (ch)
•	Slip stitch (sl st)
+	Single crochet (sc)
⊤	Half double crochet (hdc)
⊤	Double crochet (dc)

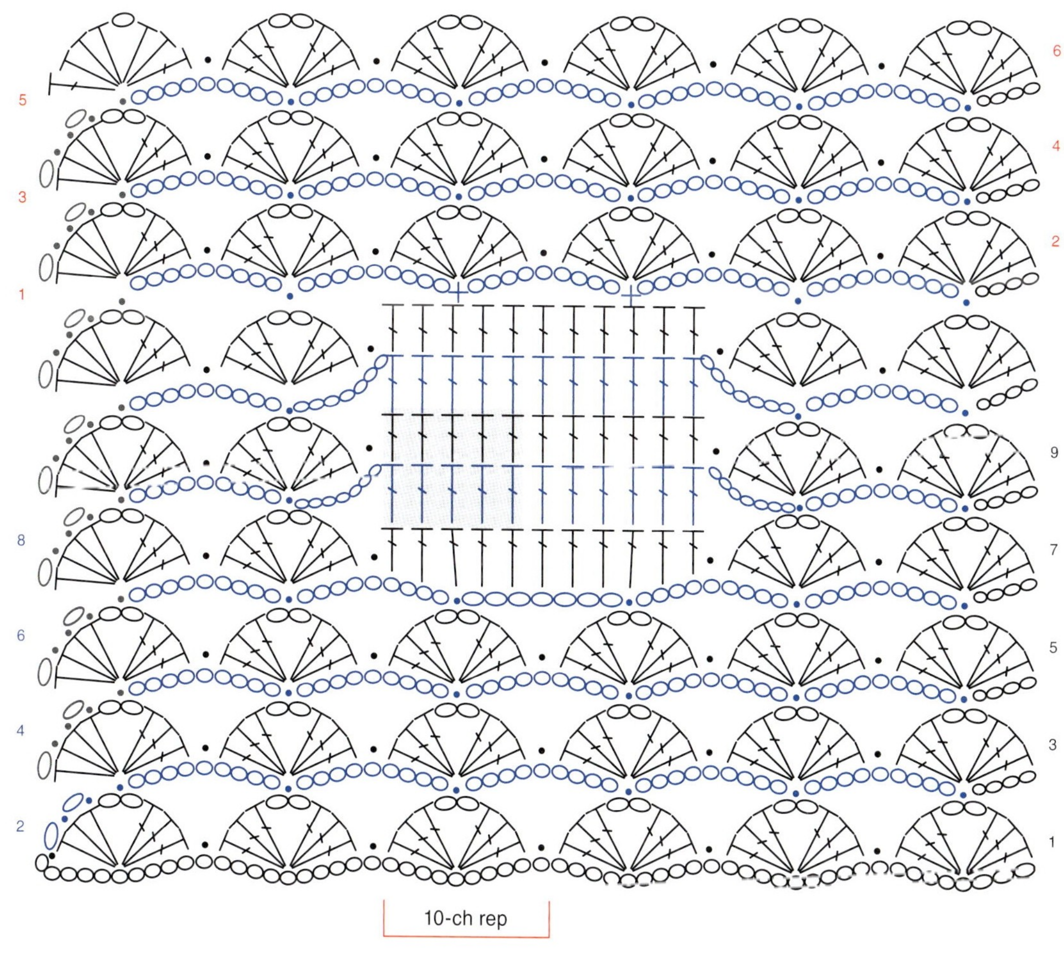

Double Crochet Shells
Stitch Diagram
Note: *Reps shown in gray.*

Large Surface Flowers

Skill Level

 **INTERMEDIATE**

Pattern Notes

Stitch markers are needed for this stitch pattern.

Foundation chain is a multiple of 7 stitches plus 6; body of swatch is a multiple of 7 stitches plus 5.

It is helpful to make these flowers in the middle of some double crochet rows before attempting to work them in the foundation chain.

Chain-3 at beginning of row counts as first double crochet unless otherwise stated.

Special Stitches

Reverse slip stitch (rev sl st): Insert hook from back to front with yarn below needle, then grab yarn with hook and pull through fabric and lp on hook.

Flower: Ch 5, 4 dc in 2 lps *(flower center)* of 4th ch from hook *(first petal made)*, on wrong side, place marker in 2 strands at base of first dc made in first petal, **rev sl st** *(see Special Stitches)* in next st on current row, ch 1, fold main work away, (sl st, ch 2, 4 dc) in same 2 lps of flower center *(2nd petal made)*, remove hook from work and straighten so live st is now above last dc worked in current row, sl st in this dc, ch 1, [(sl st, ch 2, 4 dc, ch 2) in single strand rem in flower center] twice *(3rd and 4th petals made)*, rev sl st in marked strands on WS of first petal.

Flower back: On WS of flower, sl st loosely from right to left in 2 strands near top of 4th dc of 4th petal, sl st loosely in 2 strands near top of first dc of 3rd petal.

Large Surface Flowers

Ch a multiple of 7 sts + 6 *(see Pattern Notes)*.

Row 1 (RS, start bottom border): Dc in 4th ch from hook, [work **flower** *(see Special Stitches)*, dc in next 6 ch] across to 2 chs from end, work flower, dc in last ch, turn.

Row 2: Ch 3 *(see Pattern Notes)*, [work **flower back** *(see Special Stitches)*, dc in each of next 5 unworked dc] across to last flower, work flower back, dc in last 2 dc, turn.

Row 3: Ch 3, dc in each sl st and dc across, turn.

Row 4: Ch 3, dc in each st across, turn.

Row 5 (start side borders): Ch 3, dc in next dc, work flower, dc in each st across to 2 dc from end, work flower, dc in last 2 dc, turn.

Row 6: Ch 3, work flower back, dc in each dc across to next petal, work flower back, dc in last 2 dc, turn.

[Rep rows 3–6] to desired length minus bottom border, ending with a row 4.

Next row (start top border): Ch 3, dc in next dc, [work flower, dc in each of next 6 dc] across to 2 dc from end, work flower, dc in last 2 dc, turn.

Last row: Rep row 2. Fasten off. ●

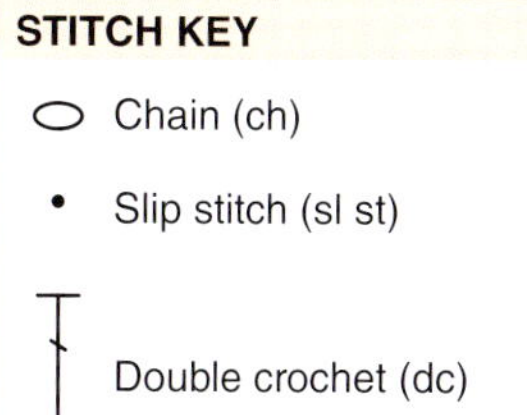

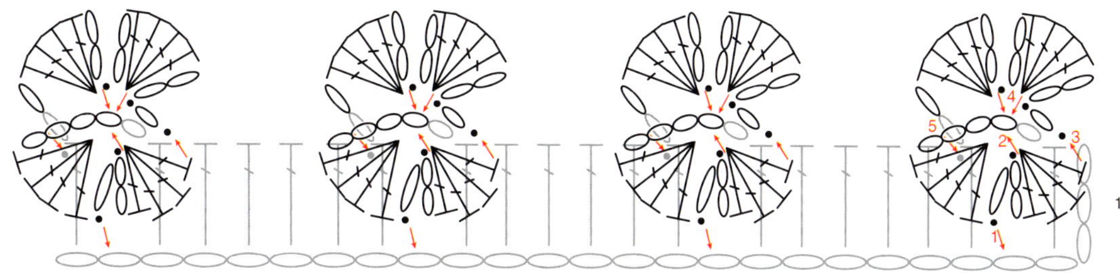

Large Surface Flowers
Bottom Border Diagram

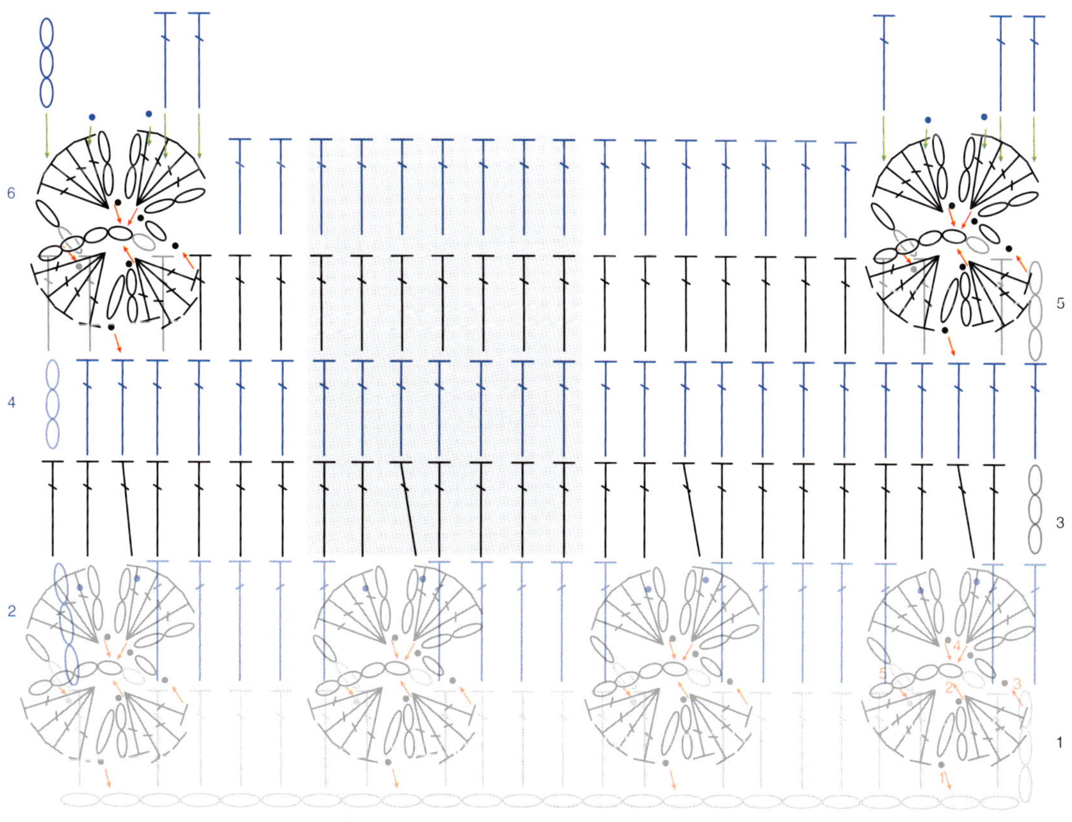

Large Surface Flowers
Stitch Diagram
***Note:** Reps shown in gray.*

Popcorn Posies

Skill Level

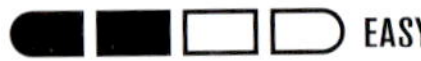 **EASY**

Pattern Note

Foundation chain is a multiple of 4 stitches plus 6; body of stitch pattern between side borders is a multiple of 4 stitches plus 1.

Special Stitches

Double crochet cluster (dc-cl): [Yo, insert hook in indicated st, yo, pull up lp, yo, pull through 2 lps on hook] twice, yo, pull through all lps on hook.

Popcorn (pc): (2 dc, **dc-cl**—*see Special Stitches*, 2 dc) in indicated st, remove hook from lp, insert hook from front to back in top of first dc and in dropped lp, draw lp through.

Posy: Fpdtr *(see Stitch Guide)* around next dc, work **pc** *(see Special Stitches)* in top of same dc, ch 1, fpdtr from right to left around same dc.

End posy: Fpdtr around next dc, work pc in top of same dc, ch 1, yo 3 times, insert hook from left to right around same dc from front to back to front, yo, pull up lp *(5 lps on hook)*, [yo, pull through 2 lps] 3 times, yo, insert hook in indicated ch of turning ch, yo, pull up lp, yo, draw through 2 lps, yo, draw through all lps on hook.

Puff: [Yo, insert hook, pull up long lp] 3 times, yo, draw through all 7 lps on hook.

Sprig: (Work **puff**—*see Special Stitches*), ch 2, work puff) in indicated st.

Popcorn Posies

Ch a multiple of 4 sts + 6 *(see Pattern Notes)*.

Row 1 (WS, start bottom border): Dc in 5th ch and in each ch across, turn.

Row 2: Ch 3, sk first dc, [work **posy** *(see Special Stitches)* in next dc, sk next dc, dc in next dc, sk next dc] across to last 3 sts, work **end posy** *(see Special Stitches)* in last dc and 2nd ch from top of turning ch.

Row 3 (start side borders): Ch 3, sk first 2 sts, [dc in next pc st, dc in each of next 3 sts, sk next ch-1] across, dc in last pc, dc in next fpdtr, sk turning ch, turn.

Row 4: Ch 3, sk first dc, work posy in next dc, sk next dc, [dc in next dc, sk next dc, work **sprig** *(see Special Stitches)* in next dc, ch 1, sk next dc] across to last 5 sts, sk next st, dc in next dc, sk next st, end posy in next st and top of ch-3, turn.

Row 5: Ch 3, sk first 2 sts, dc in next pc, dc in each of next 2 sts, [dc in next ch-1 sp, dc in next ch-2 sp, dc in 2nd ch st of same ch sp, sk next puff, dc in next dc] across, dc in next fpdtr, sk ch sp, dc in last pc, dc in next fpdtr, sk turning ch, turn.

[Rep rows 4 and 5] to desired length minus length of bottom border.

Last row (top border): Rep row 2, working end posy in last dc and top of ch-3. Fasten off. ●

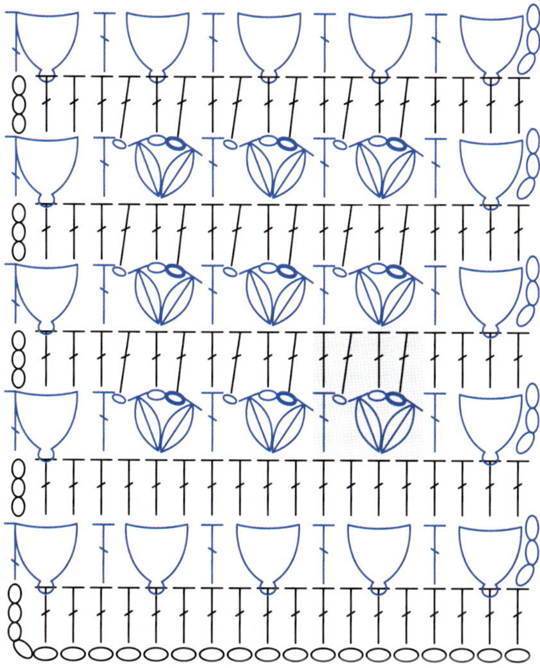

Popcorn Posies
Stitch Diagram
Note: *Reps shown in gray.*

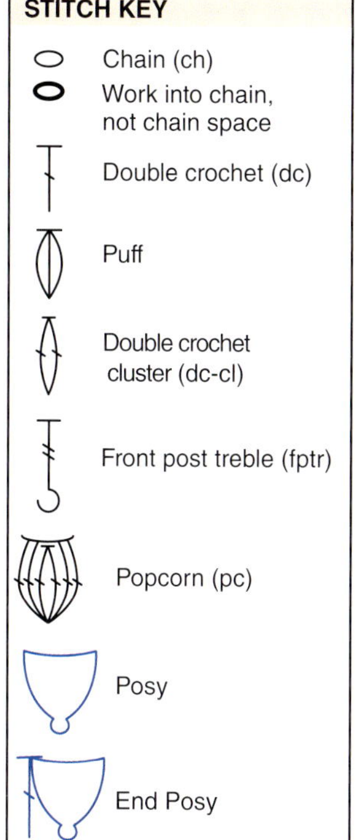

Popcorn Posies
Posy Stitch Diagram

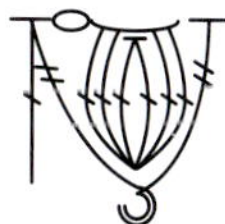

Popcorn Posies
End Posy Stitch Diagram

Popcorn Flowers

Skill Level

 INTERMEDIATE

Pattern Notes

Stitch markers are needed for this stitch pattern.

Foundation chain is a multiple of 6 stitches plus 5; body of stitch pattern is a multiple of 4 stitches plus 3.

Special Stitches

Shell: (Dc, hdc, ch 1, hdc, dc) in indicated st or sp.

Popcorn (pc): Work 5 hdc in indicated st or sp, remove hook from lp, insert hook from back to front in top of first hdc made and in dropped lp, draw lp through.

End popcorn (end pc): Hdc in indicated st or sp, mark top 2 lps of hdc just made, work 4 more hdc and complete as in pc. Do not remove marker until instructed.

Beginning shell (beg shell): Ch 5, sl st in back lp of 2nd ch from hook, (hdc, ch 1, hdc, dc) in both marked lps of pc, remove marker.

Picot: Ch 4, sl st in both lps of 4th ch from hook.

Small picot: Ch 1, sl st in front of ch-1 from right to left in 2 lps at top of last dc made.

Popcorn Flowers

Ch a multiple of 6 sts + 5 (see Pattern Notes).

Row 1 (RS, start bottom border): Sl st in back lp of 2nd ch from hook, sk next 3 chs, (tr, ch 1, 2 dc) in back lp of next ch, sk next 4 chs, [work **shell** (see Special Stitches) in both lps of next ch, sk next 5 chs] across, (2 dc, ch 1, dc, tr) in both lps of last ch, turn.

Row 2: Ch 1, sl st loosely in first 2 sts, ch 2, work **pc** (see Special Stitches) in next ch sp, [ch 5, sk next 4 sts, work pc in next ch sp] across, working **end pc** (see Special Stitches) in last ch sp, turn.

Row 3 (start side borders): Work **beg shell** (see Special Stitches), ch 1, dc in next ch sp, [dc in both lps of last ch st of same ch sp**, 3 dc in next ch sp] across, ending last rep at ** in next-to-last ch sp, dc in next ch sp, ch 1, work shell in both lps of last ch of same ch sp, sk rem of row, turn.

Row 4: Ch 1, sl st loosely in first 2 sts, ch 2, work pc in next ch sp, ch 3, sk next 3 sts, dc in next 3 dc, [**picot** (see Special Stitches), dc in next 4 dc] across to next ch sp, ch 3, sk next 3 sts, work end pc in last ch sp, turn.

Row 5: Work beg shell, ch 1, sk next ch sp, folding picots forward, dc in each dc across, ch 1, work shell in both lps of last ch of next ch sp, sk rem of row, turn.

[Rep rows 4 and 5] to desired length minus length of bottom border, ending with a row 5.

Next row (WS, start top border): Ch 1, sl st loosely in first 2 sts, ch 2, work pc in next ch sp, ch 3, sk next 3 sts, dc in next 2 dc, [work **small picot** *(see Special Stitches)*, dc in each of next 4 dc] across, ending last rep with dc in last dc, ch 3, sk next 3 sts, work end pc in last ch sp, turn.

Next row: Work beg shell, sk next ch sp and dc, [work shell in top lp only of next picot, sk next 4 dc] across, ending last rep with sk last 2 dc, (tr, dc, ch 1, 2 dc) in both lps of last ch of next ch sp, sk rem of row, turn.

Last row: Ch 1, sl st loosely in each of first 2 sts, ch 2, work pc in next ch sp, ch 6, [sk next 4 sts, work pc in next ch sp, ch 5] across, after last pc, ch 1, sl st in same sp, ch 1 to secure. Fasten off. ●

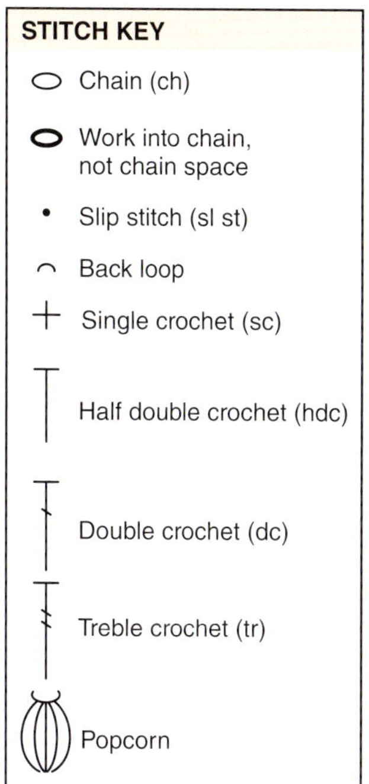

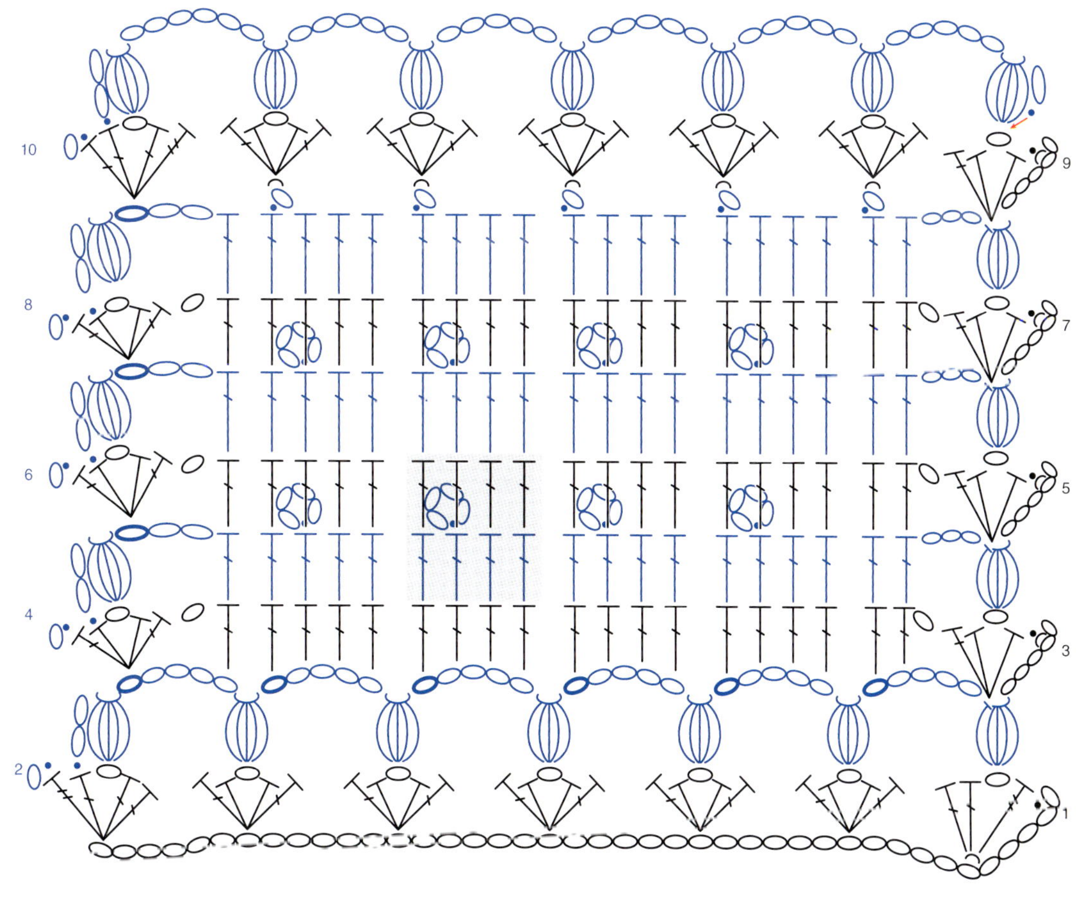

Popcorn Flowers
Stitch Diagram
Note: Reps shown in gray.

Spirals

Skill Level

 INTERMEDIATE

Pattern Notes

There is no starting chain for this pattern; the first row becomes the foundation row.

Body of stitch pattern between borders is a multiple of 4 stitches.

Chain-3 at beginning of row counts as first double crochet unless otherwise stated.

Special Stitch

Spiral: Ch 7, 4 sc in 2nd ch from hook, [3 sc in next ch] 4 times, 2 sc in last ch.

Spirals

Row 1 (bottom border): Ch 2, [**spiral** (see Special Stitch), ch 4] to desired width, do not turn.

Row 2 (RS): Ch 3 (see Pattern Notes), sk (first spiral and next ch), dc in next ch st, 2 dc in next ch st, *sk (ch, spiral, ch), 2 dc in each of next 2 sts, rep from * across to last ch-4 sp, sk (ch, spiral, ch), 2 dc in next ch st, dc in next ch st, sk last spiral, dc in last ch, turn.

Row 3 (side borders): Work spiral, ch 3, sk first dc, dc in next dc, 2 dc in next dc, *sk 2 dc, 2 dc in each of next 2 dc, rep from * across to last 5 sts, sk 2 dc, 2 dc in next st, dc in each of last 2 sts, turn.

Rep row 3 to desired length minus length of bottom border, ending with a WS row.

Last row (top border): Work spiral, ch 2, [**dc dec** (see Stitch Guide) in next 2 sts twice, work spiral] across, sc in 2nd ch of last ch-3. Fasten off. ●

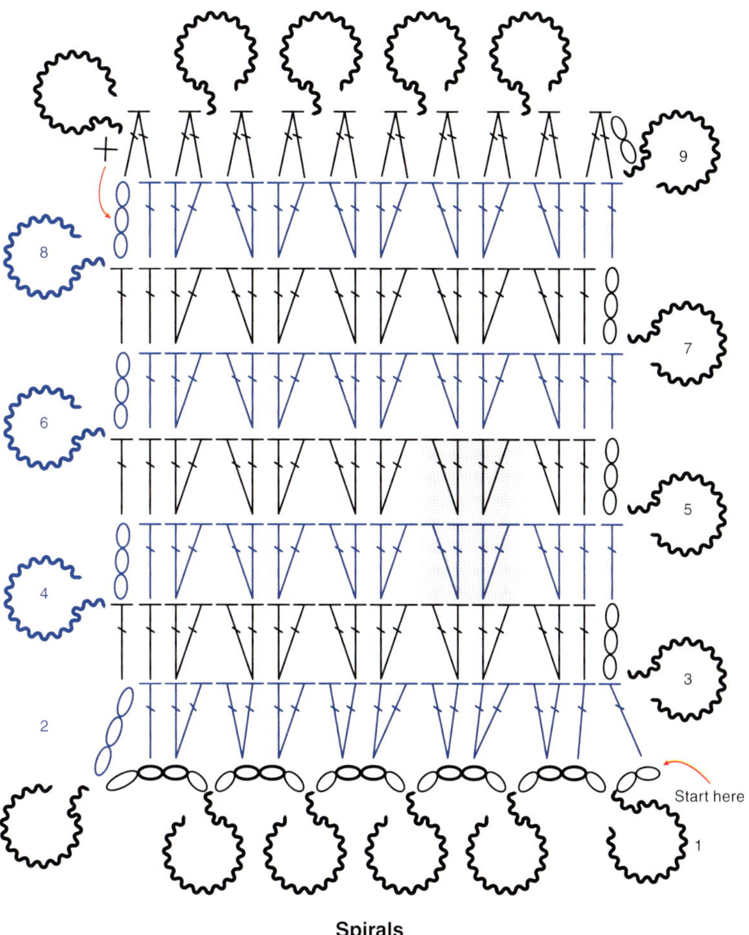

Spirals
Stitch Diagram
Note: Reps shown in gray.

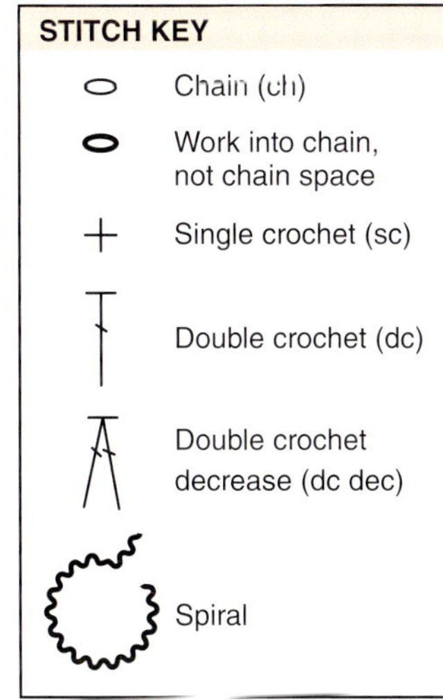

STITCH KEY

⬭	Chain (ch)
⬮	Work into chain, not chain space
+	Single crochet (sc)
⊤	Double crochet (dc)
⅄	Double crochet decrease (dc dec)
〰	Spiral

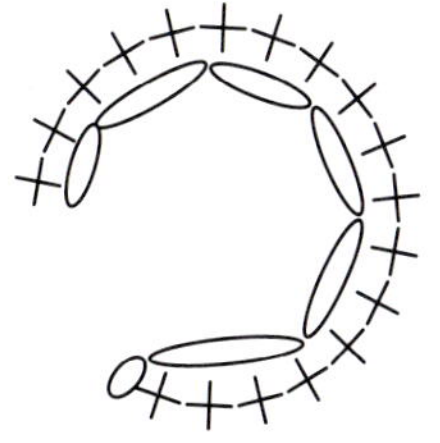

Spirals
Spiral Stitch Diagram

Layered Fans

Skill Level

 **EXPERIENCED**

Pattern Notes

Stitch markers are needed for this stitch pattern.

There is no starting chain for this pattern; the first row becomes the foundation row.

If fans "cup" too much, such as with tighter or stiffer yarns, simply add 1 or 2 double crochet stitches to the indicated number of stitches in eye of each fan.

When working double crochet stitches for fan around post of first double crochet, ensure the first time the hook is inserted that there are 3 strands of yarn on the stitch to the right of the hook.

Body of stitch pattern between borders has a multiple of 4 stitches plus 3.

First corner fan will be tacked to first side fan after work is complete to avoid borders being pulled out of alignment.

No turning chains are worked before side fans or top fans.

Slip stitches in top row should be worked tightly.

Special Stitches

Corner fan: Dc in 2nd ch from hook, ch 3, work 13 dc around post of dc just made.

Half fan: Dc in 2nd ch from hook, ch 3, work 11 dc around post of dc just made.

Special front post double crochet (special fpdc): Working around indicated horizontal dc, insert hook in sp between 2 top lps and 3rd vertical strand, yo, pull up lp, [yo, draw through 2 lps on hook] twice.

Anchoring back post double crochet (anchoring bpdc): Yo, insert hook from back to front under both lps of ch at top of indicated beg ch and from front to back, under both lps of next dc, then insert hook under lower post of indicated dc, yo, pull up lp through all layers, [yo, pull through 2 lps] twice.

Reverse slip stitch (rev sl st): With RS of work facing, sl st from back to front in indicated lp or st.

Side fan: Dc in first dc, rotate work counterclockwise, ch 2, rev sl st in **front lp** (see Stitch Guide) of marked dc at base of first dc, rotate work clockwise, 11 dc around post of last dc made.

Short treble (short tr): Yo twice, insert hook in indicated st or sp, pull up lp, yo, draw through 2 lps on hook, yo, draw through all 3 lps on hook.

Top fan: Dc in same dc as last sl st made, ch 2, **rev sl st** (see Special Stitches) around side of 2nd of 2 dc just sk by inserting hook between 2 top lps and 3rd vertical strand, 11 dc around post of dc just made.

"/>

Layered Fans

Row 1 (RS, bottom border): Ch 2, work **corner fan** *(see Special Stitches)*, *ch 5, work **half fan** *(see Special Stitches)*, place marker in top of ch-3, rep from * to 1 half fan width less than desired width of piece, including borders, ch 5, corner fan, mark beg ch-3 of fan just made, do not turn.

Row 2: Being careful not to twist, rotate work to continue back along fans just made;

A. dc around first ch-3 strand between fans, place marker in dc just made, **special fpdc** *(see Special Stitches)* in **first dc of next fan** *(see Pattern Notes)*, **anchoring bpdc** *(see Special Stitches)* in beg ch-3 of corner fan and around first horizontal dc of next fan already worked in, remove marker;

B. dc in eye of same fan as last 2 dc made, *dc around next ch-3 strand between fans, special fpdc in first dc of next fan, anchoring bpdc in beg ch-3 of previous fan and around dc of next fan already worked, remove marker**, dc in eye of same fan, rep from *, ending last rep at **;

C. when first dc of corner fan has been worked, sk remainder of row, turn, **leaving corner fan unworked** *(see Pattern Notes)*.

Row 3 (WS, side borders): Do not make turning ch *(see Pattern Notes)*, dc in first dc, ch 3, work 11 dc around post of last dc made, dc in occupied first dc of row, mark dc just made, dc in **back lp** *(see Stitch Guide)* of each dc across to st before next marked dc, 2 dc in both lps of next dc, turn, leaving rem sts unworked.

Row 4: Dc in first dc, rotate work counterclockwise, ch 2, **rev sl st** *(see Special Stitches)* in marked st 2 rows below, rotate work clockwise, 11 dc around post of last dc made, dc in occupied first dc, move marker to dc just made, dc in back lp of each dc across to next marked dc, dc in both lps of next dc, turn, leaving rem sts unworked.

Row 5: Work **side fan** *(see Special Stitches)*, dc in occupied first dc, move marker to st just made, dc in back lp of each dc across to next marked dc, dc in both lps of next dc, turn, leaving rem sts unworked.

Rep row 5 to desired length minus length of bottom border, ending with a RS row.

Top Border

Note: *See rows numbered in pink on Stitch Diagram for Top Border rows.*

Row 1: Work side fan, mark base of last dc made in fan, dc in occupied first dc, move marker to st just made, dc in back lp of each dc across to 1 dc before next marked dc, **short tr** *(see Special Stitches)* in next dc, tr in marked dc, turn, leaving rem sts unworked.

Row 2: Dc in first tr, ch 4, rev sl st in 1 strand only of base of marked dc, remove marker, 2 tr around post of last dc made, mark first tr just made, 4 dc, short tr, 2 tr, short tr, dc) around same post, sk first occupied st of row, **sl st** *(see Pattern Notes)* in next st, dc in same st as last sl st made, ch 2, rev sl st in 1 strand only of base of marked tr, remove marker, work 11 dc around post of last dc made, [sk next 2 dc, sl st in each of next 2 dc, work **top fan** *(see Special Stitches)*] across to marked st, sk marked st and first st of next side fan, work top fan, sl st to 1 strand at base of same side fan dc. Fasten off.

Finishing

Loosely tack marked bottom fan to the side fan above it to secure, remove markers. ●

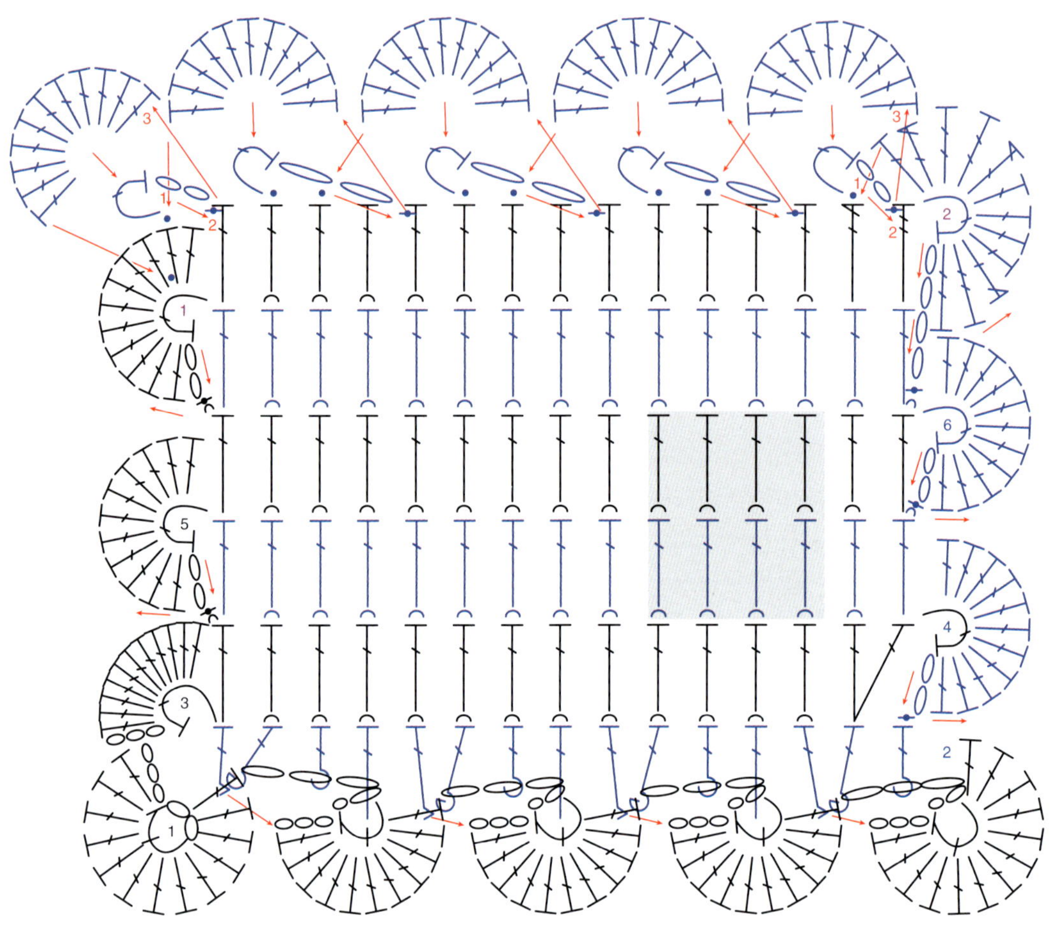

Layered Fans
Stitch Diagram
Note: *Reps shown in gray.*

STITCH KEY

- Slip stitch (sl st)
- Reverse slip stitch (rev sl st)
- Chain (ch)
- Double crochet (dc)
- Double crochet whose post forms ring for fan
- Back loop
- Front post double crochet (fpdc)
- Short treble
- Special front post double crochet (special fpdc)
- Anchoring back post double crochet (anchoring bpdc)

Daisy Chain

Skill Level

 INTERMEDIATE

Pattern Notes

Foundation chain is a multiple of 5 stitches plus 4.

Where indicated, work into both back bump and back loop of chain together from underside of chain stitch.

Daisy eyelets are formed in the strand under the chain nearest a cluster or extended half double crochet stitch.

Special Stitches

Extended cluster (ext cl): Yo, insert hook in indicated st, yo, pull up lp, yo, draw through first lp on hook and lengthen lp to height of row, sk indicated number of sts, yo, insert hook in next indicated st, yo, pull up lp, yo draw through first lp on hook and lengthen lp to height of row, yo, draw through 5 lps on hook.

Y-stitch (Y-st): [Yo, insert hook in next st, yo, pull up lp, yo, draw through first lp on hook] twice, yo, draw through first 3 lps on hook, [yo, draw through 2 lps on hook] twice.

Picot: Ch 3, insert hook under back bump and back lp of 3rd ch from hook, yo, draw up lp, yo, draw through both lps on hook.

Extended half double crochet (ext hdc): Yo, insert hook in indicated st, yo, pull up lp, yo, draw through first lp on hook and lengthen to height of row, yo, draw through 3 lps on hook.

Wide extended shell (wide ext shell): (**Ext hdc** *(see Special Stitches)*, ch 3, ext hdc) in indicated st.

Extended shell (ext shell): (Ext hdc, ch 2, ext hdc) in indicated st.

Daisy Chain

Ch a multiple of 5 sts + 4 *(see Pattern Notes)*.

Row 1 (RS, start bottom border): Sc in **back bump and back lp** *(see Pattern Notes)* of 3rd ch from hook, ch 4, **ext cl** *(see Special Stitches)* with first leg going in same st as sc just made, sk 3 chs, 2nd leg in next ch, *ch 3, ext cl with first leg going in next ch, sk 3 chs, 2nd leg in next ch, rep from * across to last 2 chs, ch 3, **Y-st** *(see Special Stitches)* in last 2 sts, turn.

Row 2: Picot *(see Special Stitches)*, ch 2, **wide ext shell** *(see Special Stitches)* in juncture of **ch closest to next ext cl** *(see Pattern Notes)*, [**ext shell** *(see Special Stitches)* in each juncture of ch closest to next ext cl] across to last ext cl, wide ext shell in last ext cl, ch 1, dc in 3rd ch from hook, turn.

Row 3: Picot, ch 3, ext cl with first leg in next ext hdc, sk (ch-3, ext hdc), 2nd leg in next ext hdc, ch 4, *2 dc in next ch-2 sp, dc in sp between next 2 shells, rep from * across to last ch-2 sp, 2 dc in last ch-2 sp, ch 3, ext cl with first leg in next ext hdc, sk ch-3, 2nd leg in next ext hdc, ch 4, dc in 2nd ch of last ch-2, turn.

Row 4: Picot, ch 2, wide ext shell in next ext cl, ch 1, dc in each dc across, wide ext shell in next ext cl, ch 1, dc in 3rd ch from hook.

Row 5: Picot, ch 2, wide ext shell in juncture of ch closest to next ext cl, ch 1, dc in each dc across to ch sp, wide ext shell in next ext cl, ch 1, sk 2 chs, dc in next ch, turn.

[Rep rows 4 and 5] to desired length minus length of bottom border, ending with a row 4.

Top Border

Note: *See rows numbered in red on Stitch Diagram for Top Border rows.*

Row 1: Picot, ch 3, ext cl with first leg in next ext hdc and 2nd leg in next ext hdc, ch 3, *ext cl with first leg in same st as last st worked, sk 2 dc, 2nd leg in next dc, ch 3, rep from * across to last 2 dc, ext cl with first leg in same st as last st worked, 2nd leg in next ext hdc, ch 3, ext cl with first leg in same st just worked, 2nd leg in next ext hdc, ch 4, dc in 2nd ch of last ch-2, turn.

Row 2: Ch 1, picot, wide ext shell in each ext cl across, ch 1, tr in 3rd ch from hook. Fasten off. ●

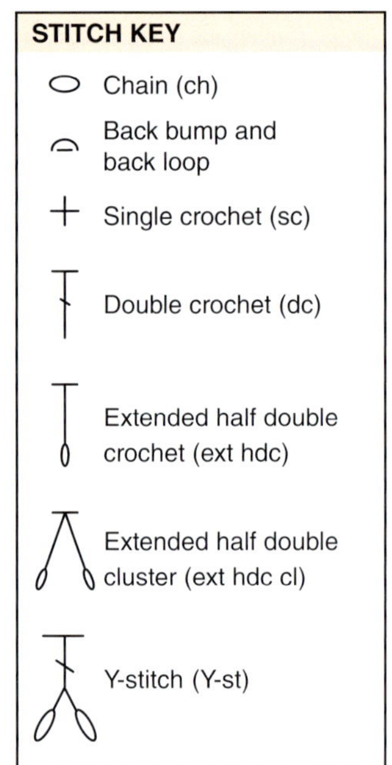

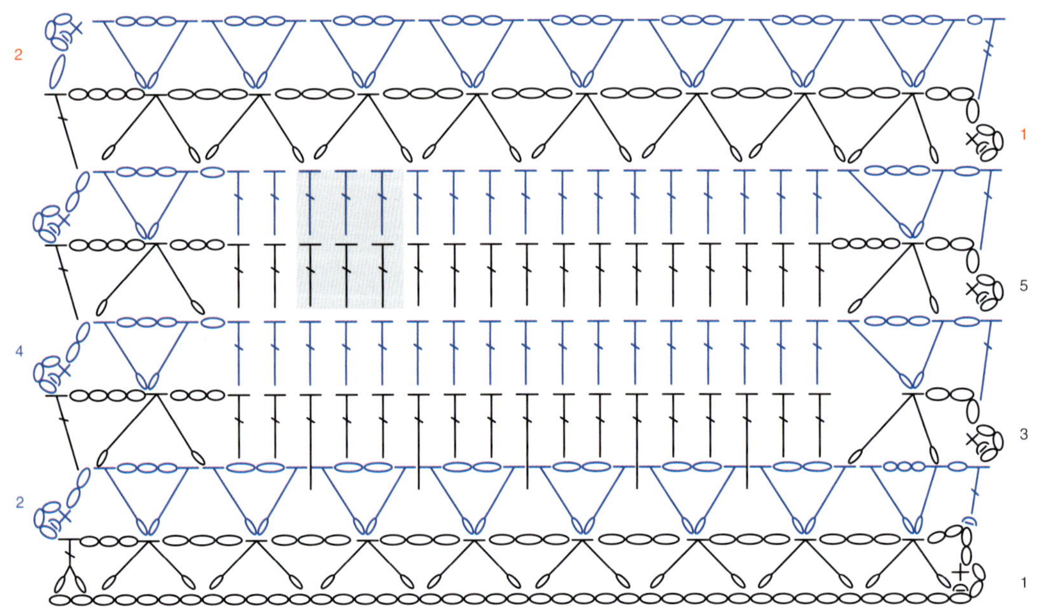

Daisy Chain
Stitch Diagram
Note: *Reps shown in gray.*

Tight Chain Braids

Skill Level

■■■□ INTERMEDIATE

Pattern Notes

Body of stitch pattern between borders is an even number of stitches.

Use 6 different-colored markers and take note of which color corresponds to which braid plait.

Fold plaits down to right side of fabric when not used for braiding.

Turning chains are not counted as stitches.

Special Stitch

V-stitch (V-st): 2 dc between indicated pair of dc sts.

Special Technique

Lower braid: Working on RS, and working from left to right, ignore plaits marked as side border, fold right-hand side of marked beg bottom border plait forward and to left, without twisting rem of plaits, pull next plait through first twisted plait, [pull each plait through the plait to the left] across, including last marked bottom border plait through previous plait, keep next marked side border plait on WS of bottom border braid, with WS facing, insert hook in dropped working lps, yo, insert hook in back lp of last sc and through last bottom border plait, taking care not to twist the latter, yo, pull up strand loosely through plait and sc, yo, draw through 2 lps on hook, yo, draw through all 3 lps on hook, remove bottom border markers only, turn.

Tight Chain Braids

Ch 21.

Row 1 (RS, start bottom border): Sc loosely in 2nd ch from hook, working normally throughout, ch 13, sc in next ch, mark plait just made as beg plait of side border, ch 12, sc in each of next 2 chs, mark plait just made as last plait of bottom border, [ch 12, sc in each of next 2 sc] across to last 4 chs, ch 12, sc in next ch, sl st in next ch, ch 12, sc in next ch, mark last plait made as beg plait of bottom border braid, ch 15, hdc in last ch, mark last plait made as beg of side border, turn.

Row 2 (lower braid): Ch 15, sl st in **back lp only** *(see Stitch Guide)* of 13th ch from hook, mark the 2 free lps of same ch st, mark plait just made as 2nd plait of side border, keeping plaits to front of fabric throughout, sk (first hdc, sc and next sl st), 2 dc in next sc, dc in each sc across to last 2 sc, ch 12, sl st in 1 lp only of 12th ch from hook, work dc to 2 lps left on hook in next sc, place live lps on marker, remove hook from lps. Work **lower braid** *(see Special Technique)*.

Row 3 (start side borders): Ch 2, dc in first st, ch 12, sl st in **front lp only** *(see Stitch Guide)* of 12th ch from hook, sk next plait, dc in next dc, [2 dc in next dc *(counts as V-st)*, sk next dc] across to last 2 dc, dc in next dc, ch 12, sl st in 1 lp only of 12th ch from hook, sk last dc, dc in marked lps of ch st of next side plait from previous row, remove this marker, turn.

Row 4: Ch 15, sl st in back lp only of 13th ch from hook, mark 2 free lps of same ch, sk first dc and next plait, dc in next dc, [work **V-st** *(see Special Stitches)* between next 2 dc] across until 3 sts rem after last V-st, sk next dc, dc in next dc, ch 12, sl st in 1 lp only of 12th ch from hook, sk next plait, dc in last dc, leave turning ch unworked, turn.

Row 5: Ch 2, dc in first dc, ch 12, sl st in front lp only of 12th ch from hook, sk next plait, dc in next dc, [work V-st between next 2 dc] across until 3 sts rem after last V-st, sk next dc, dc in next dc, ch 12, sl st in front lp only of 12th ch from hook, sk next dc, dc in marked lps of ch st of next plait, remove this marker, turn.

[Rep rows 4 and 5] to desired length minus length of bottom border, ending with a row 4.

Next row (start top border): Rep row 5 except ch 10 and sl st in 10th ch from hook for both plaits.

Next row: Ch 3, sk first dc, skipping both plaits, dc in next dc, [work V-st between next 2 dc] across until 3 sts rem after last V-st, sk next dc, dc in each of next 2 sts, leaving turning ch unworked, turn.

Next row (side braids): Ch 2, **braid right-edge border plaits tog by working from bottom, fold right-hand side of marked beg border plait forward and to left, without twisting rem plaits, pull each plait through the plait above it to top**, sc in last plait pulled up, hdc in first dc, (sc, ch 12, sc) in next dc, sc in next dc, [ch 12, sc in each of next 2 dc] across to last 2 dc, ch 12, sc dec over next 2 dc *(counts as 1 sc)*, sc in top ch of turning ch, folding left-hand side of only marked beg border plait forward and to right, rep from ** to ** to braid left-edge border plaits tog, sc in last plait pulled up, remove markers, ch 13, working behind top border plait, hdc in same turning ch as next-to-last sc made, turn.

Last row: Ch 1 loosely, sk first hdc, sl st loosely in sc in top-side border plait, sk plaits throughout, sc in next and each sc across to next hdc, working rem of sl sts loosely, sl st in next hdc, sl st in next sc in plait.

Top braid: Working on RS from left to right, fold left-hand side of first plait forward and to right, without twisting rem of plaits, braid plaits tog in same manner as bottom border plaits, with WS facing, sl st in top of ch-2 turning ch and through last plait tog, ch 1 to secure. Fasten off. ●

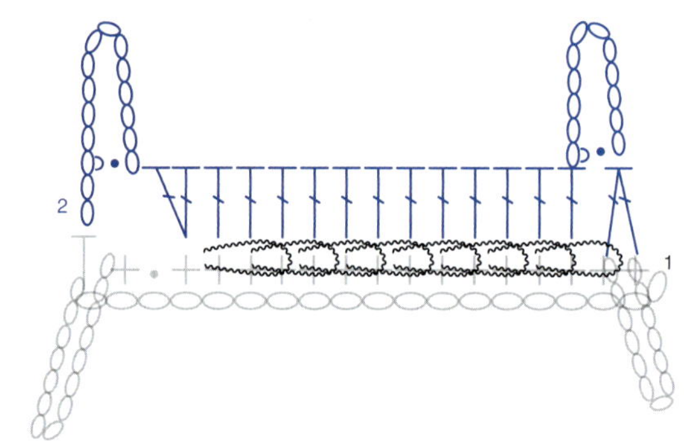

Tight Chain Braids
Stitch Diagram

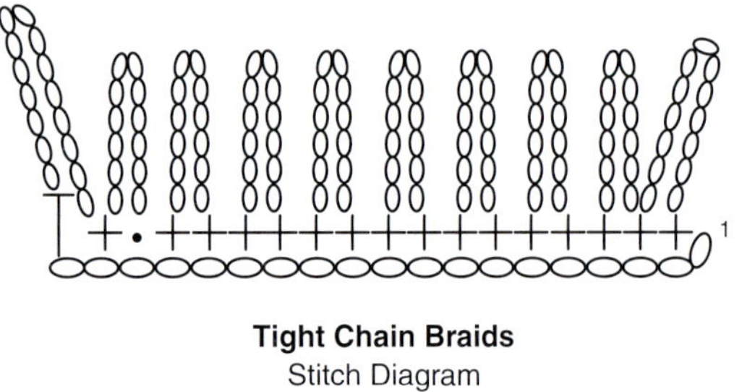

Tight Chain Braids
Stitch Diagram

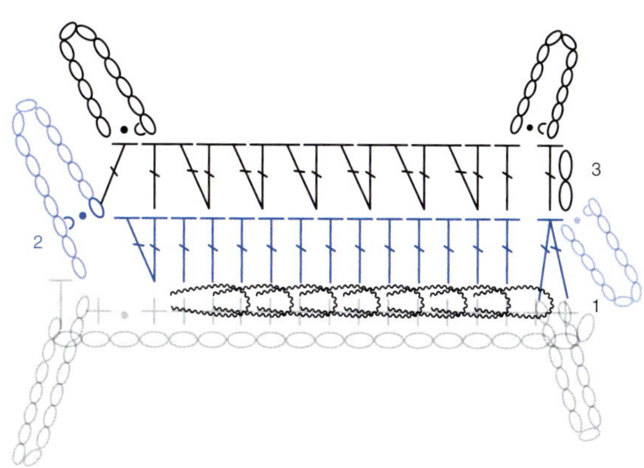

Tight Chain Braids
Stitch Diagram

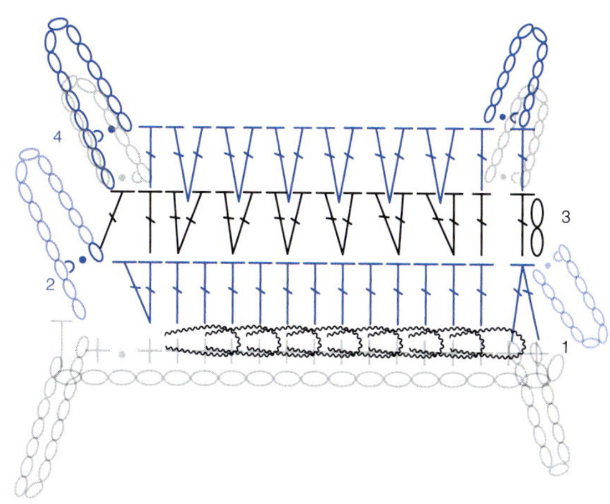

Tight Chain Braids
Stitch Diagram

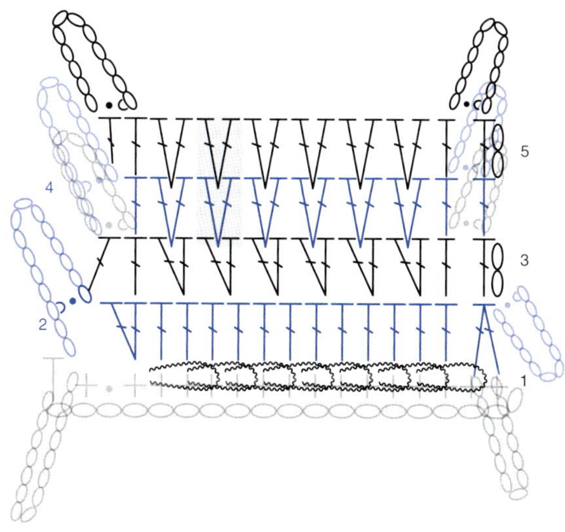

Tight Chain Braids
Stitch Diagram
Note: *Reps shown in gray.*

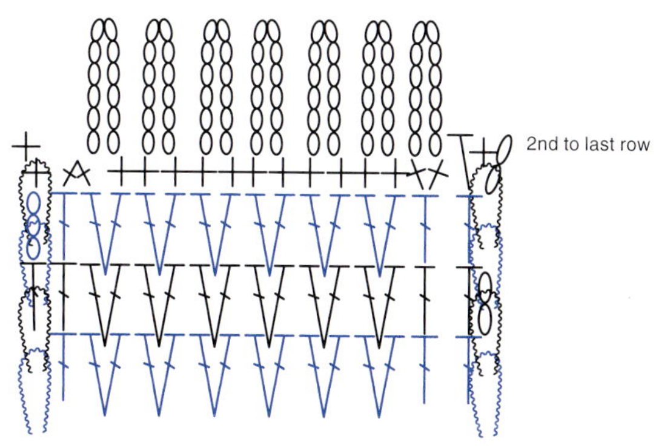

Tight Chain Braids
Stitch Diagram

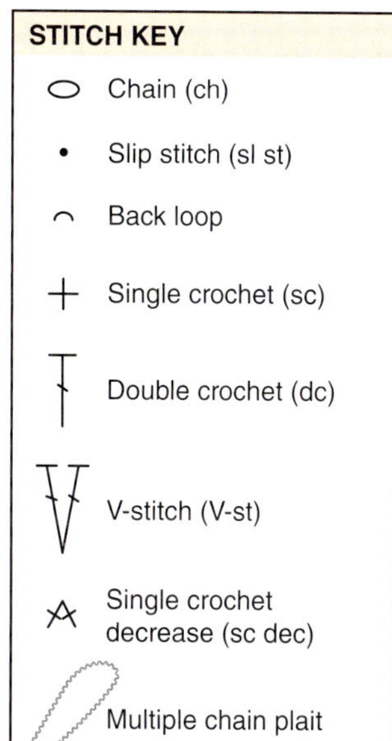

STITCH KEY

⬯	Chain (ch)
•	Slip stitch (sl st)
⌒	Back loop
+	Single crochet (sc)
┬	Double crochet (dc)
V	V-stitch (V-st)
⋏	Single crochet decrease (sc dec)
⬭	Multiple chain plait

Crossed Posts 1

Skill Level

 INTERMEDIATE

Pattern Notes

Foundation chain is a multiple of 2 stitches plus 3.

Chain-3 at beginning of row counts as first double crochet unless otherwise stated.

Special Stitches

Front cluster (front cl): Yo 4 times, insert hook from front to back to front around indicated st in lower row, yo, pull up lp, [yo, draw through 2 lps] 4 times, yo, insert hook in next indicated st in current row, yo, pull up lp, yo, pull through 2 lps, yo, pull through all 3 lps on hook

Right edge: Sk next 2 sts, bptr around turning ch, dc in 2nd skipped st in front of last bptr made, bptr from right to left around first sk st.

Crossed double crochet (xdc): Sk next st, dc in next dc, ch 1 *(does not count as st, ignore in subsequent rows)*, working behind last dc made, dc in sk dc.

Left edge: Sk next 2 sts, fptr around turning ch, dc in 2nd sk st behind last fptr made, fptr around first sk st.

Crossed Posts 1

Ch a multiple of 2 sts + 3 *(see Pattern Notes)*.

Row 1 (RS, start bottom border): Sc in 3rd ch from hook, [ch 2, sk next ch, sc in next ch] across to 3rd ch from end, sl st in last ch, turn.

Row 2: Ch 3 *(see Pattern Notes)*, dc in first sc, dc in next ch-2 sp, [dc in next sc, dc in next ch-2 sp] across to last sc, sk ch-1 sp on foundation ch, **bptr** *(see Stitch Guide)* in last ch-2 sp of foundation ch, dc in last sc of current row, bptr in sk ch-2 sp, turn.

Row 3: Ch 3, dc in next dc, **fptr** *(see Special Stitches)* around next st, sk ch sp in foundation ch already worked, fpdtr around next ch sp in foundation ch, *sk dc on current row, **front cl** *(see Special Stitches)* with first leg in sk ch sp and dc in next st on current row, rep from * across to last 3 sts, sk next dc on current row, **fpdtr** *(see Special Stitches)* in last ch sp of foundation ch, dc in next dc on current row, fpdtr in 2nd to last ch sp of foundation row, sk turning ch, turn.

Row 4 (start side borders): Ch 3, dc in next dc, bptr around next tr, dc in each st across to last 3 sts, work **right edge** *(see Special Stitches)*, turn.

Row 5: Ch 3, dc in next dc, fptr around next st, dc in each of next 2 sts, **xdc** *(see Special Stitches)* across to last 5 sts, dc in each of next 2 dc, work **left edge** *(see Special Stitches)*, turn.

Row 6: Ch 3, dc in next dc, bptr around next tr, dc in each of next 2 dc, xdc across to last 5 sts, dc in each of next 2 dc, work right edge, turn.

[Rep rows 5 and 6] to desired length minus length of bottom border, ending with a row 5.

Top Border

Note: See rows numbered in red on Stitch Diagram for Top Border rows.

Row 1: Ch 3, dc in next dc, bptr around next tr, dc in each dc across to last 3 sts, work right edge, turn.

Row 2: Ch 3, dc in next dc, fptr around next st, dc in each dc across to last 3 sts, work left edge, turn.

Row 3: Ch 3, dc in next dc, bptr around next tr, dc in each dc across to last 3 sts, work right edge, turn.

Row 4: Ch 3, dc in next dc, fptr around next tr, front cl around sts from 2 rows below across to last 3 sts, sk next 2 sts, fptr around turning ch, dc in next tr behind last fptr made, keeping last lp of each st on hook, dc in next dc, fptr around occupied tr before dc just worked in, yo, draw through all 3 lps on hook. Fasten off. ●

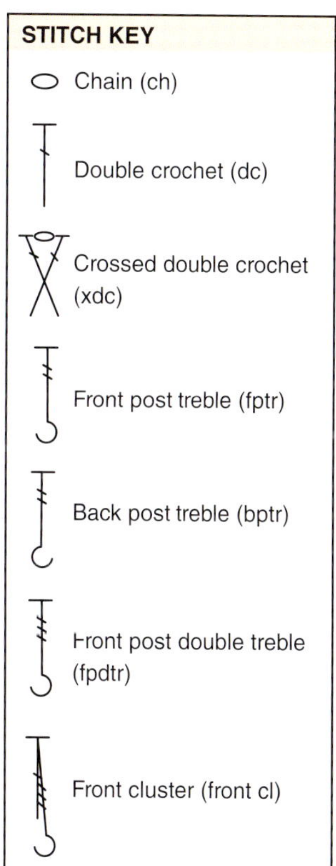

Crossed Posts 1
Stitch Diagram
Note: Reps shown in gray.

STITCH KEY

◯ Chain (ch)

| Double crochet (dc)

⟩⟨ Crossed double crochet (xdc)

Front post treble (fptr)

Back post treble (bptr)

Front post double treble (fpdtr)

Front cluster (front cl)

Crossed Posts 2

Skill Level

■■■□ INTERMEDIATE

Pattern Note

Foundation chain is a multiple of 2 stitches plus 3.

Special Stitches

Low cluster (low cl): Yo twice, insert hook from back to front to back around indicated st, yo, pull up lp, [yo, draw through 2 lps] twice *(2 lps on hook)*, yo, insert hook in indicated st, yo, pull up lp, yo, draw through 2 lps, yo, draw through all 3 lps on hook.

Front cluster (front cl): Yo 4 times, insert hook from front to back to front around indicated st in lower row, yo, pull up lp, [yo, draw through 2 lps] 5 times, yo, insert hook in next indicated st in current row, yo, pull up lp, yo, pull through 2 lps, yo, pull through all 3 lps on hook

Back cluster (back cl): Yo 4 times, insert hook from back to front to back around indicated st in lower row, yo, pull up lp, [yo, draw through 2 lps] 5 times, yo, insert hook in next indicated st in current row, yo, pull up lp, yo, pull through 2 lps, yo, pull through all 3 lps on hook

Crossed post stitches (cp sts): Sk next st on current row, sk next fptrtr from 2 rows below, fptrtr around next fptrtr from 2 rows below, **front cl** *(see Special Stitches)* around sk fptrtr and in next dc on current row.

Crossed Posts 2

Ch a multiple of 2 sts + 3 *(see Pattern Note)*.

Row 1 (RS, start bottom border): Sc in 3rd ch from hook, [ch 2, sk next ch, sc in next ch] across to 3rd ch from end, sl st in last ch, turn.

Row 2: Ch 3, dc in first sc, dc in next ch-2 sp, [dc in next sc, dc in next ch-2 sp] across to last sc, **bptr** *(see Stitch Guide)* around base ch below ch-2 sp just worked, **low cl** *(see Special Stitches)* with tr leg in ch-2 turning ch and dc leg in last sc, turn.

Row 3: Ch 3, sk first st, dc in tr, [sk next st, **fptrtr** *(see Stitch Guide)* around base ch just worked, **front cl** *(see Special Stitches)*] across, leave ch-3 unworked.

Row 4: Ch 3, dc in first st, dc in each st across to last 2 dc, **bptrtr** *(see Stitch Guide)* around last tr from row 2, sk 1 st, **back cl** *(see Special Stitches)* around sk tr from row 2 and in last dc on current row, turn.

Row 5: Ch 3, dc in next st, **cp sts** *(see Special Stitches)* across to last dc, fptrtr around last trtr from 2 rows below, front cl around sk trtr and in last dc from current row, turn.

Row 6 (start side borders): Ch 3, sk first st, dc in next st and in each st across to last dc, bptrtr around last tr from 2 rows below, back cl around sk tr from 2 rows below and in last dc on current row, turn.

Row 7: Ch 3, dc in next st, work cp sts 2 times, dc in each st across to last 5 dc, cp sts 2 times, sk trtr from 2 rows below, fptrtr around last trtr from 2 rows below, front cl around sk trtr and in last dc from current row, turn.

[Rep rows 6 and 7] to desired length minus length of bottom border, ending with a row 6.

Top Border

Note: *See rows numbered in red on Stitch Diagram for Top Border rows.*

Row 1: Ch 3, dc in next st, cp sts 2 times, cp sts around dc sts from 2 rows below across to last 6 sts, cp sts 2 times, sk trtr from 2 rows below, fptrtr around last trtr from 2 rows below, front cl around sk trtr and in last dc from current row, turn.

Row 2: Rep row 6.

Row 3: Ch 3, dc in first st, **fptr** *(see Stitch Guide)* around next st on current row, dc in same st, cp sts in each pair of sts across, turn. Fasten off. ●

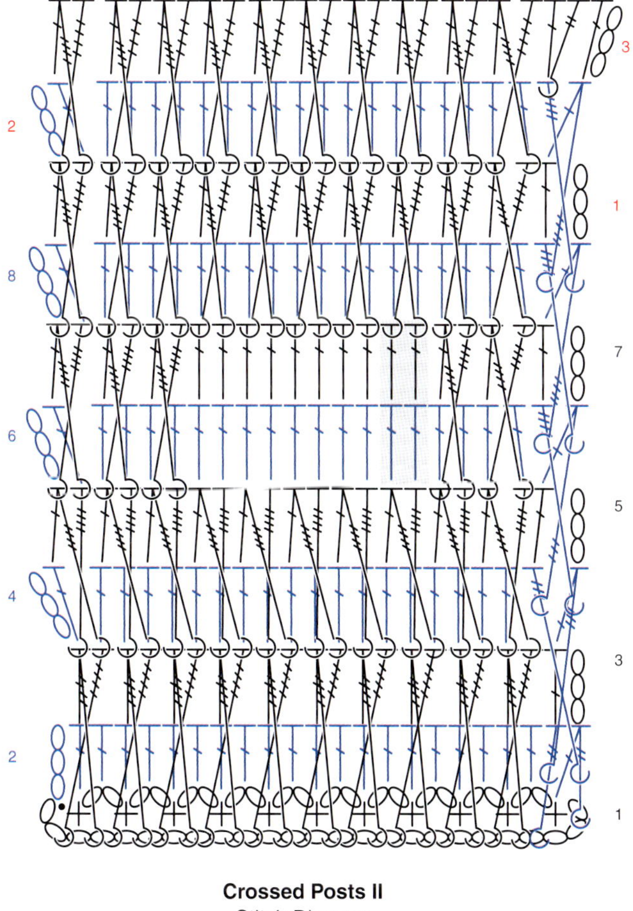

Crossed Posts II
Stitch Diagram
Note: *Reps shown in gray.*

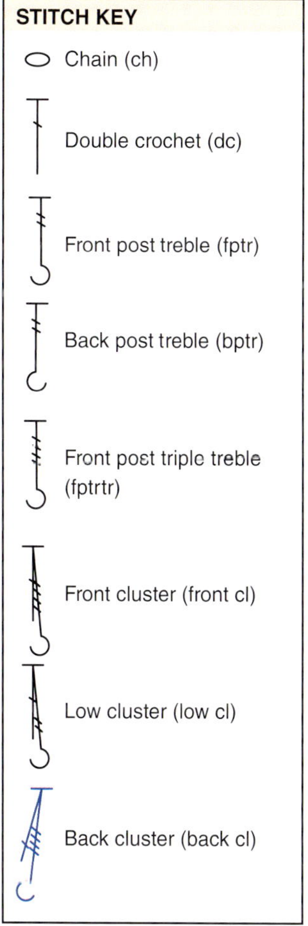

Popcorn Blossoms

Skill Level

INTERMEDIATE

Pattern Notes

Stitch markers are needed for this stitch pattern.

Foundation chain is a multiple of 6 stitches plus 7 and should be worked loosely; body of stitch pattern between borders is a multiple of 6 stitches plus 2.

First and last popcorns of first row are meant to automatically fold approximately in half, to make strong corners. When weaving in tail, encourage corner popcorn to fold.

From row 3 on, when working in any chain, insert hook in top 2 loops, not under back bar of chain unless otherwise stated.

Special Stitches

4-double crochet (5-double crochet) popcorn (4-dc [5-dc] pc): Work 4 (5) dc in indicated st, remove hook from lp, insert hook from front to back or from back to front in top of first dc made and in dropped lp, draw lp through.

Modified 4-double crochet (5-double crochet) popcorn (modified 4-dc [5-dc] pc): Work 4 (5) dc in indicated st, remove hook from lp, insert hook from front to back in top 2 lps (not under ridge lp) of last ch-1 made and in dropped lp, draw lp through. Mark these 2 top lps.

Beginning back popcorn (beg back pc): Ch 3, sk first pc st, work 4 dc in indicated st, remove hook from lp, insert hook from back to front in top of ch-3 and in dropped lp, draw lp through.

Popcorn Blossoms

Ch a multiple of 6 sts + 7 *(see Pattern Notes).*

Row 1 (RS, start bottom border): 3 dc in 3rd ch from hook, remove hook from lp, insert hook from front to back in top of first dc made (not in the turning ch) and in dropped lp, draw lp through, dc in same ch, ch 1, mark top 2 lps of ch just made, sk next 2 chs, work **4-dc pc** *(see Special Stitches)* in next ch, [ch 3, dc in each of next 2 dc, ch 1, work 4-dc pc in next ch, ch 1**, sk next 2 chs, work **modified 4-dc pc** *(see Special Stitches)* in next ch] across, ending last rep at ** 4 chs from end, sk next 2 chs, 4 dc in 2nd ch from end, remove hook from lp, insert hook from front to back in top of 2nd dc made and in dropped lp, draw lp through, dc in same ch, sk last ch, turn.

Row 2: Ch 3, sk first 3 sts, inserting hook under facing ridge and front (top) lps (not in top 2 lps), work 4 dc in next ch, remove hook from lp, insert hook from back to front in top of ch-3 and in dropped lp, draw lp through, ch 3, work 4-dc pc in same place, *ch 1, sk next pc, dc in next ch-1 sp, dc in next dc, sk (next dc, ch sp, and pc st), work (**5-dc pc**—*see Special Stitches*, ch 3, 4-dc pc) in both lps of next marked ch, remove marker, rep from * across, sk rem of row, turn.

Row 3: Ch 1, sk first pc st, [3 hdc in next ch sp, hdc in last ch of same ch sp (at top of pc), sk next pc st**, dc in each of next 2 dc, sk next ch sp and pc st] across, ending last rep at **, turn.

Row 4: Ch 1, sc in each of first 4 hdc, [dc in each of next 2 dc, sc in each of next 4 hdc] across, turn.

Row 5 (start side borders): Ch 3, work 4-dc pc in first sc, ch 1, sk next 2 sc, work **modified 5-dc pc** *(see Special Stitches)* in next sc, [ch 3, dc in each of next 2 dc, ch 1, work 4-dc pc in next sc, ch 1, sk next 2 sc, work modified 4-dc pc in next sc] across, turn.

Row 6: Work (**beg back pc**—*see Special Stitches*, ch 3, 4-dc pc) in both lps of next marked ch, remove marker, *ch 1, sk next pc, dc in next ch-1 sp, dc in next dc, sk (next dc, ch sp, and pc), work (5-dc pc, ch 3, 4-dc pc) in both lps of next marked ch, remove marker, rep from * across, turn.

[Rep rows 3–6] to desired length minus bottom border.

Last row: Work (beg back pc, ch 3, 4-dc pc) in both lps of next marked ch, remove marker, *ch 1, sk next pc, dc in next ch-1 sp, dc in next dc, sk (next dc, ch sp, and pc st)**, work (5-dc pc, ch 3, 4-dc pc) in both lps of next marked ch, remove marker, rep from * across, ending at **, work 5-dc pc in last marked ch, remove marker, ch 3, work 4-dc pc in **back lp only** *(see Stitch Guide)* of same ch, ch 2, sl st in both lps of next pc st. Fasten off. ●

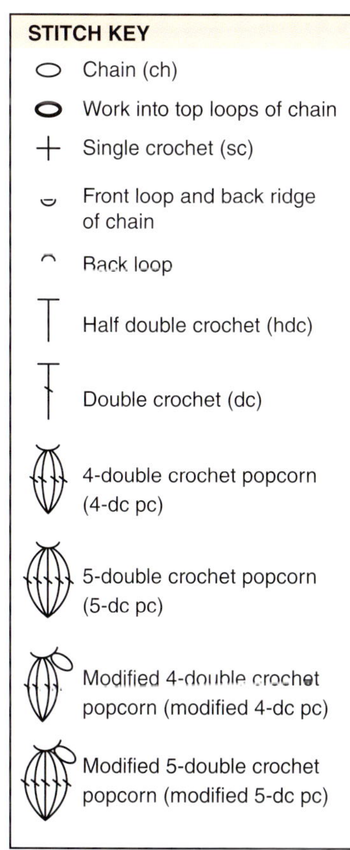

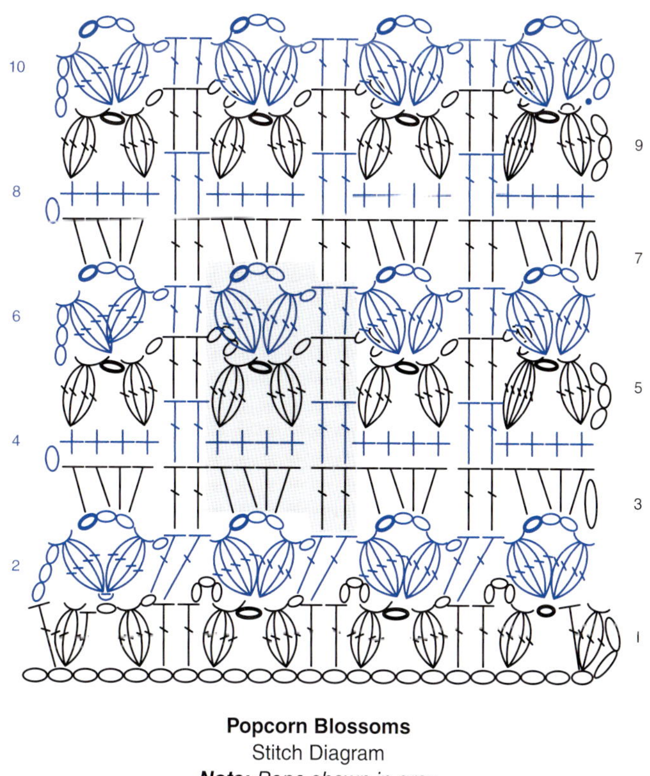

Popcorn Blossoms
Stitch Diagram
Note: Reps shown in gray.

Large Surface Leaves

 **INTERMEDIATE**

Pattern Notes

Foundation chain is a multiple of 5 stitches plus 4.

Chain-3 at beginning of row counts as first double crochet unless otherwise stated.

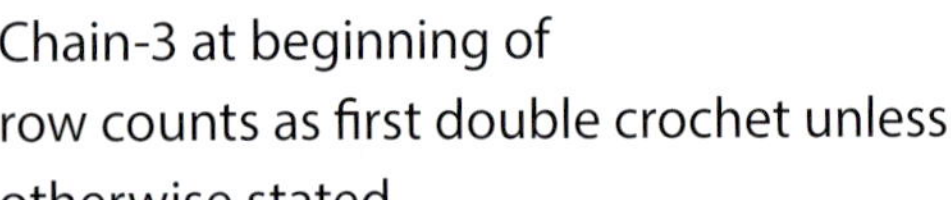

Special Stitches

Leaf: Yo 5 times, folding work back as necessary, insert hook normally in both lps of indicated st, yo, pull up lp, [yo, draw through 2 lps on hook] 5 times *(2 lps on hook)*, yo 4 times, *insert hook from front in both lowest diagonal strand and vertical strand right below it in last post made, yo, pull up lp**, [yo, draw through 2 lps on hook] 4 times *(3 lps on hook)*, yo 3 times, rep from * to **, [yo, draw through 2 lps on hook] 3 times *(4 lps on hook)*, yo, insert hook in next skipped dc on current row, yo, pull up lp, yo, draw through 2 lps on hook, yo, draw through all 5 lps on hook.

Left edge leaf: In sk st 2 rows below, yo 5 times, folding work back as necessary, insert hook normally in both lps of indicated st, yo, pull up lp, [yo, draw through 2 lps on hook] 5 times *(2 lps on hook)*, yo 4 times, *insert hook from front in both lowest diagonal strand and vertical strand right below it in last post made, yo, pull up lp**, [yo, draw through 2 lps on hook] 4 times *(3 lps on hook)*, yo 3 times, rep from * to **, [yo, draw through 2 lps on hook] 3 times *(4 lps on hook)*, yo, insert hook in same st as last dc made on current row, yo, pull up lp, yo, draw through all 6 lps on hook.

Leaflet: Working on RS, [yo, insert hook from right to left around post of indicated dc, yo, pull up long lp] twice, yo, draw through 4 lps on hook, yo, draw through 2 lps on hook.

Large Surface Leaves

Ch a multiple of 5 sts + 4 *(see Pattern Notes)*.

Row 1 (RS, start bottom border): Dc in 5th ch from hook, sk next ch, 2 dc in next ch, dc in next ch, sk next ch, 2 dc in next ch, [dc in each of next 3 chs, sk next ch, 2 dc in next ch] across to last 4 chs, dc in next ch, sk next ch, 2 dc in next ch, dc in last ch, turn.

Row 2: Ch 3 *(see Pattern Notes)*, dc in each dc across, turn.

Row 3: Ch 2, completing **leaf** *(see Special Stitches)* in first dc of current row, work leaf in next sk ch 2 rows below, dc in same dc on current row, [dc in each of next 4 dc, work leaf in next sk ch 2 rows below] across to last 5 sts, dc in next 5 sts, work **left edge leaf** *(see Special Stitches)*, turn.

Row 4 (start side borders): Ch 3, sk first 2 sts, dc in each st across to last leaf, sk leaf st, turn.

Row 5: Ch 3, sk first dc, dc in next dc, sk next dc, 2 dc in next dc, dc in each of next 3 dc, [sk next dc, work **leaflet** *(see Special Stitches)* around next dc, dc in same dc, dc in each of next 3 dc] across to last 4 sts, dc in next dc, sk next dc, 2 dc in next dc, dc in last dc, turn.

Row 6: Rep row 2.

Row 7: Ch 2, completing leaf in first dc of current row, work leaf in next sk dc 2 rows below, dc in same dc in current row, dc in each of next 3 dc, [sk next dc, work leaflet around next dc, dc in same dc, dc in each of next 3 dc] across to last 2 dc, dc in each of next 2 dc, work left edge leaf, turn.

[Rep rows 4–7] to desired length minus length of bottom border, ending with a row 4.

Top Border

Note: See rows numbered in red on Stitch Diagram for Top Border rows.

Row 1: Ch 3, sk first dc, [dc in next dc, sk next dc, 2 dc in next dc] twice, [dc in each of next 3 dc, sk next dc, 2 dc in next dc] across to last 4 sts, dc in next dc, sk next dc, 2 dc in next dc, dc in last st, turn.

Row 2: Ch 3, sk first dc, dc in next and each dc across, turn.

Row 3: Working leaves in sk dc sts 2 rows below, rep row 3. Fasten off. ●

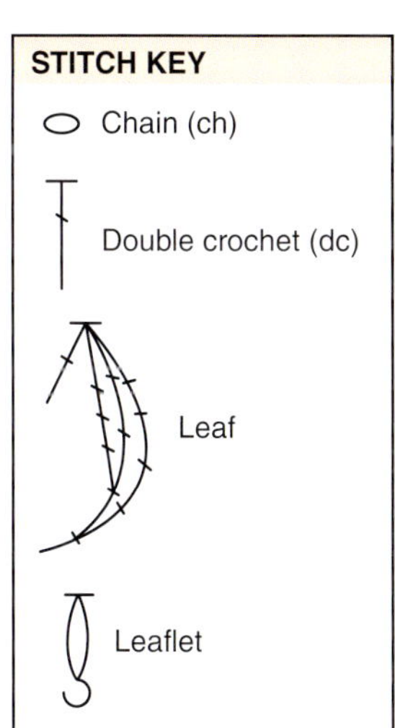

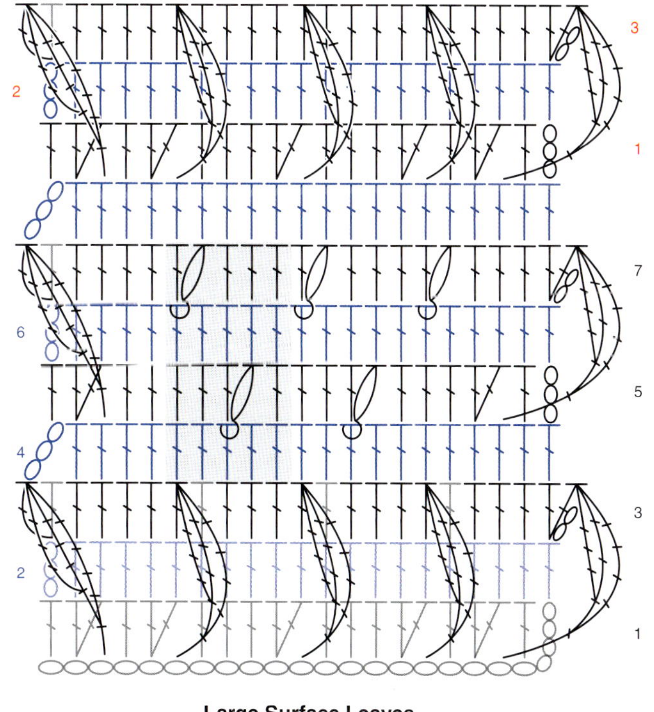

Large Surface Leaves
Stitch Diagram
Note: Reps shown in gray.

Wicker Lace 1

Skill Level

 INTERMEDIATE

Pattern Notes

Foundation chain is a multiple of 18 stiches plus 6; body of stitch pattern between side borders is a multiple of 14 stitches.

Chain-2 at beginning of odd rows plus the next chain worked counts as first double crochet unless otherwise stated.

Special Stitches

Lace motif B: Ch 2, sc in next ch-4 sp, ch 3, sc in next ch-4 sp, ch 2, dc in next dc.

Lace motif A: Ch 4, dc in next sc twice, ch 4, dc in next dc.

V-stitch (V-st): Work 2 dc in gap between indicated dc sts.

Wicker Lace 1

Ch a multiple of 18 sts + 6 *(see Pattern Notes).*

Row 1 (start bottom border): Dc in 9th ch from hook *(4th–6th chs count as first dc)*, sk 2 chs, dc in next ch, ch 4, sk 2 chs, dc in next ch, *ch 4, sk 2 chs, dc in next ch, sk 2 chs, dc in next ch, ch 4, sk 2 chs, dc in next ch, rep from * across, turn.

Row 2: Ch 3, work **lace motif B** *(see Special Stitches)* 4 times.

Row 3: Ch 2 *(see Pattern Notes),* work **lace motif A** *(see Special Stitches)* 4 times.

Row 4: Rep row 2.

Row 5: Ch 2, work lace motif A once, [2 dc in next ch sp, 3 dc in next ch sp, 2 dc in next ch sp] twice, dc in next dc, work lace motif A once, turn.

Row 6 (start side borders): Ch 3, work lace motif B once, dc in each of next 2 dc, *2 dc in next dc, sk next dc, rep from * across to 3 sts before next ch sp, dc in each of the next 3 sts, work lace motif B once, turn.

Row 7: Ch 2, work lace motif A once, dc in each of next 2 dc, [**V-st** *(see Special Stitches)* between next 2 sts, sk 2 dc] across to 3 dc before ch sp, dc in each of next 3 dc, work lace motif A once, turn.

Row 8: Ch 3, work lace motif B once, dc in each of next 2 dc, V-st in each V-st across to 3 dc before next ch sp, dc in each of next 3 dc, work lace motif B once, turn.

[Rep rows 7 and 8] to desired length minus Top Border, ending with a row 7.

Top Border

Note: *See rows numbered in red on Stitch Diagram for Top Border rows.*

Row 1: Ch 3, work lace motif B once, dc in each dc across to ch sp, work lace motif B once, turn.

Row 2: Ch 2, work lace motif A once, *ch 4, [sk 2 dc, dc in next dc] twice, ch 4**, sk 2 dc, dc in gap between last sk dc and next dc, rep from * to 8 sts before next ch sp, ending at **, ch 4, [sk 2 dc, dc in next dc] twice, ch 4, sk 2 dc, dc in each of next 2 dc, work lace motif A once, turn.

Rows 3–5: Rep bottom border rows 2–4. Fasten off. ●

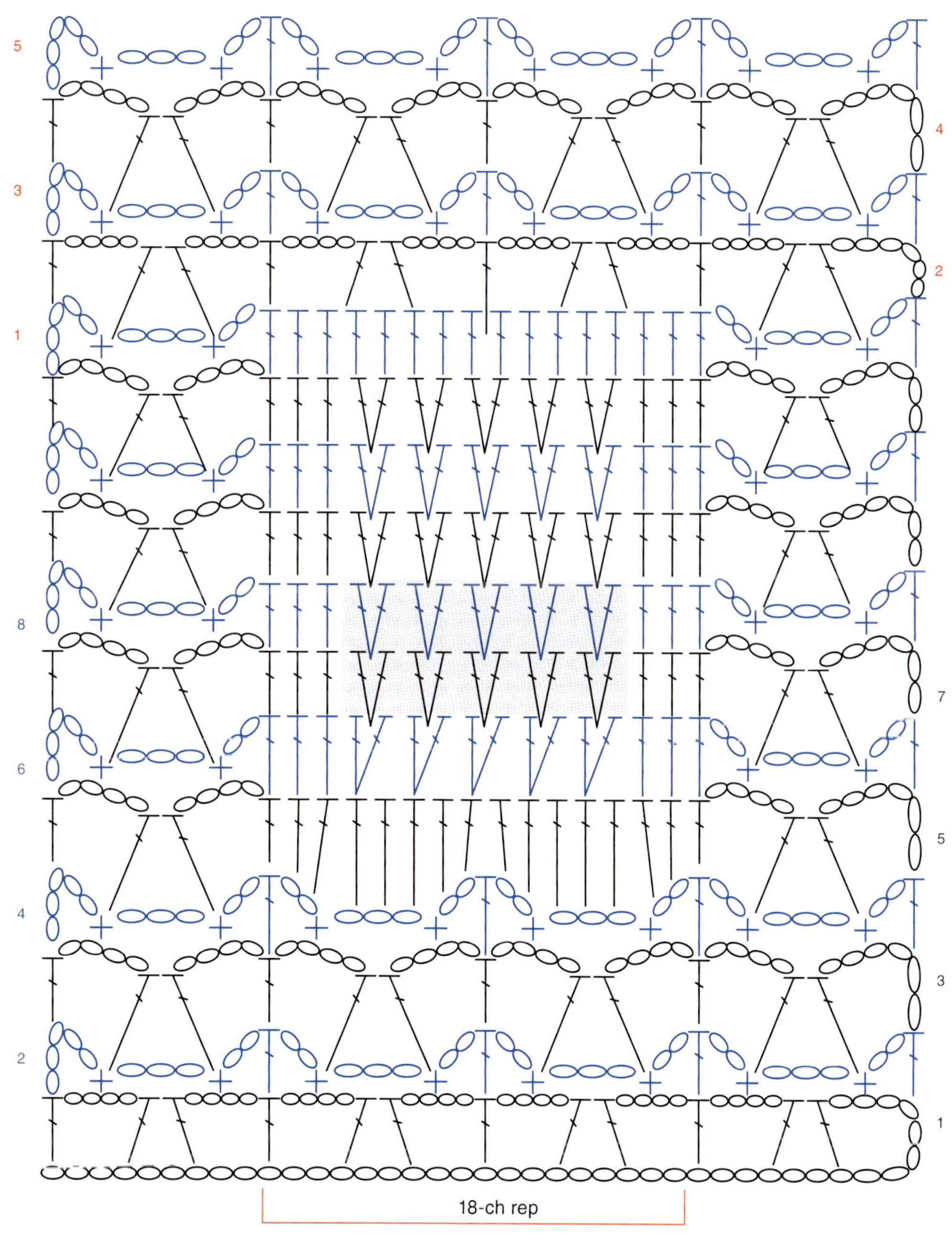

Wicker Lace 1
Stitch Diagram
Note: Reps shown in gray.

Wicker Lace 2

Skill Level

■■■□ **INTERMEDIATE**

Pattern Notes

Foundation chain is a multiple of 9 stitches plus 6; body of stitch pattern between side borders is a multiple of 9 stitches plus 3.

Chain-3 at beginning of row counts as first double crochet unless otherwise stated.

Special Stitches

Lace motif A: Ch 4, sk next st, dc in next st, sk 2 sts, dc in next st, ch 4, sk next st, dc in each of next 3 sts.

Cinch motif: Ch 2, sc in next ch sp, ch 3, sc in next ch sp, ch 2, dc in each of next 3 dc.

Lace motif B: Ch 4, dc in each of next 2 sc, ch 4, dc in each of next 3 dc.

Full motif: 3 dc in each of next 2 ch sps, dc in each of next 3 dc.

Decrease (dec): Dc dec *(see Stitch Guide)* in 3 sts by skipping middle st or ch sp.

Shell: (Dc, ch 2, dc) in indicated st.

Wicker Lace 2

Ch a multiple of 9 sts + 6 *(see Pattern Notes)*.

Row 1 (start bottom border): Dc in 5th ch from hook and in each ch across, turn. *(39 dc)*

Row 2: Ch 3 *(see Pattern Notes)*, dc in each of next 2 sts, work **lace motif A** *(see Special Stitches)* 4 times across, turn.

Row 3: Ch 3, dc in each of next 2 sts, work **cinch motif** *(see Special Stitches)* 4 times across, turn.

Row 4: Ch 3, dc in each of next 2 sts, work **lace motif B** *(see Special Stitches)* 4 times across, turn.

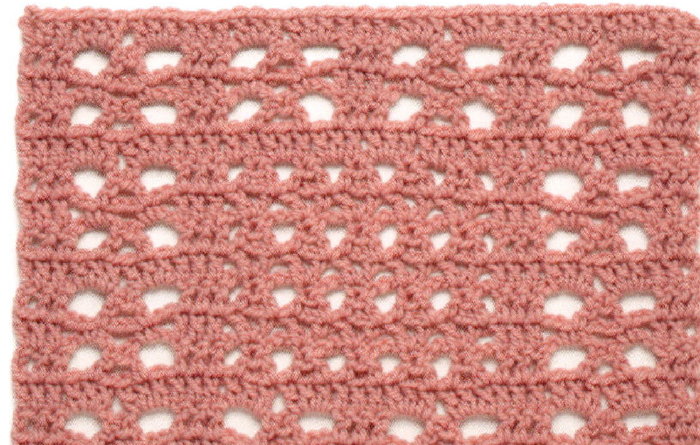

Row 5: Ch 3, dc in each of next 2 sts, work **full motif** *(see Special Stitches)* 4 times across, turn.

Row 6 (start side borders): Ch 3, dc in each of next 2 sts, work lace motif A once, ch 2, [**dec** *(see Special Stitches)*, ch 3] across to last 12 sts, ch 2, dc in each of next 3 sts, work lace motif A once, turn.

Row 7: Ch 3, dc in each of next 2 sts, work cinch motif once, **shell** *(see Special Stitches)* in each dec across, dc in each of next 3 sts, work cinch motif once, turn.

Row 8: Ch 3, dc in each of next 2 sts, work lace motif B once, ch 2, [dec in next shell, ch 3] across to side border, dc in each of next 3 sts, work lace motif B once, turn.

Row 9: Ch 3, dc in each of next 2 sts, work full motif, shell in each dec across, dc in each of next 3 dc, work full motif, turn.

[Rep rows 6–9] to desired length minus bottom border, ending with a row 7.

Top Border

Note: *See rows numbered in red on Stitch Diagram for Top Border rows.*

Row 1: Ch 3, dc in each of next 2 sts, work lace motif B, ch 2, [dec in next shell, ch 2] across to side border, dc in each of next 3 dc, work lace motif B once, turn.

Row 2: Ch 3, dc in each of next 2 sts, work full motif once, dc in next ch sp, [dc in next dec**, 2 dc in next ch sp] across to last dec, ending last rep at **, dc in last ch-2 sp, dc in each of next 3 dc, work full motif once, turn.

Rows 3–6: Rep bottom border rows 2–5. Fasten off. ●

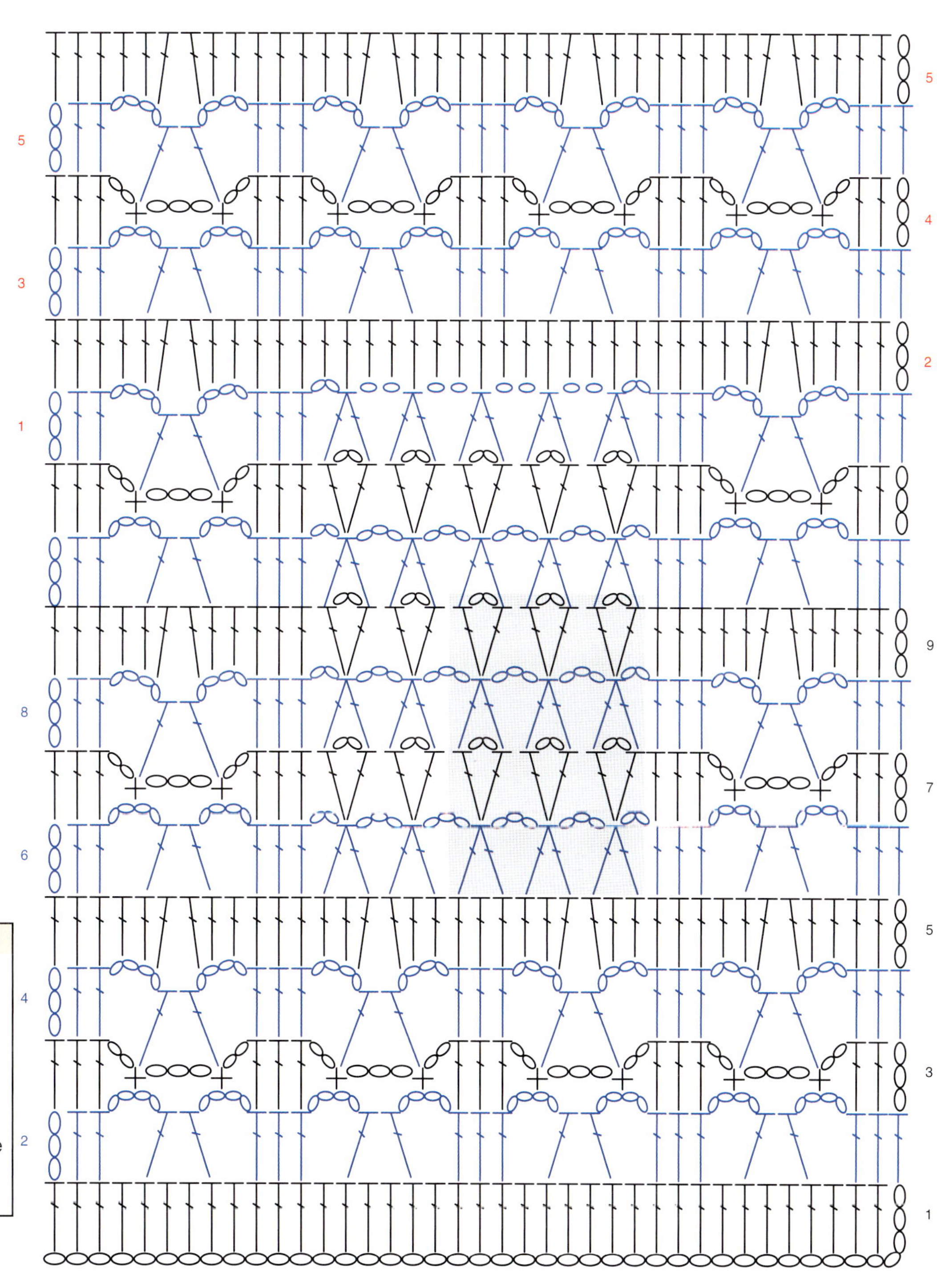

STITCH KEY

⬭ Chain (ch)

+ Single crochet (sc)

┬ Double crochet (dc)

⋀ Double crochet decrease (dc dec)

Wicker Lace 2
Stitch Diagram
Note: *Reps shown in gray.*

Banner Tabs

Skill Level

◼◼◼▢ INTERMEDIATE

Pattern Notes

Stitch markers are needed for this stitch pattern.

Body of stitch pattern between side borders is a multiple of 4 stitches plus 2.

When working into chains for tabs, with underside of chain facing, insert hook under back bump and back loop.

Remove stitch markers as you work into marked stitches.

Special Stitch

Tab: Ch 6, sl st in 2nd **ch** *(see Pattern Notes)* from hook, sc in next ch, hdc in next ch, dc in each of next 2 chs.

Banner Tabs

Row 1 (start bottom border): Ch 1, work **tab** *(see Special Stitch)*, dc in next ch *(3 dc made)*, *place marker around post of last dc worked and place 2nd marker around post of same dc between top 2 lps of st and next horizontal strand*, [ch 8, work tab, dc in next ch, rep between *, sk next ch], rep between [ ] until desired width, excluding borders, is achieved, do not turn.

Row 2 (RS, start side borders): Work tab, 2 dc in marked edge of last dc of last tab from row 1, **remove markers** *(see Pattern Notes)*, [2 dc in next ch-1 sp, 2 dc around post of next dc] across to last marked post, dc around only 2nd marked st edge, hdc in same ch as marked dc is worked, turn.

Row 3: Work tab, dc in next hdc, dc in next dc, [2 dc in next dc, sk next dc] across to last 5 dc including sk dc, dc in 2nd and 3rd dc from hook, turn.

Rep row 3 to desired length minus bottom border, excluding borders.

Last row (start top border): Work tab, sk first 2 sts, [sl st loosely in next 2 dc, work tab, sk next 2 dc] across to last tab, sl st in dc before last tab. Fasten off. ●

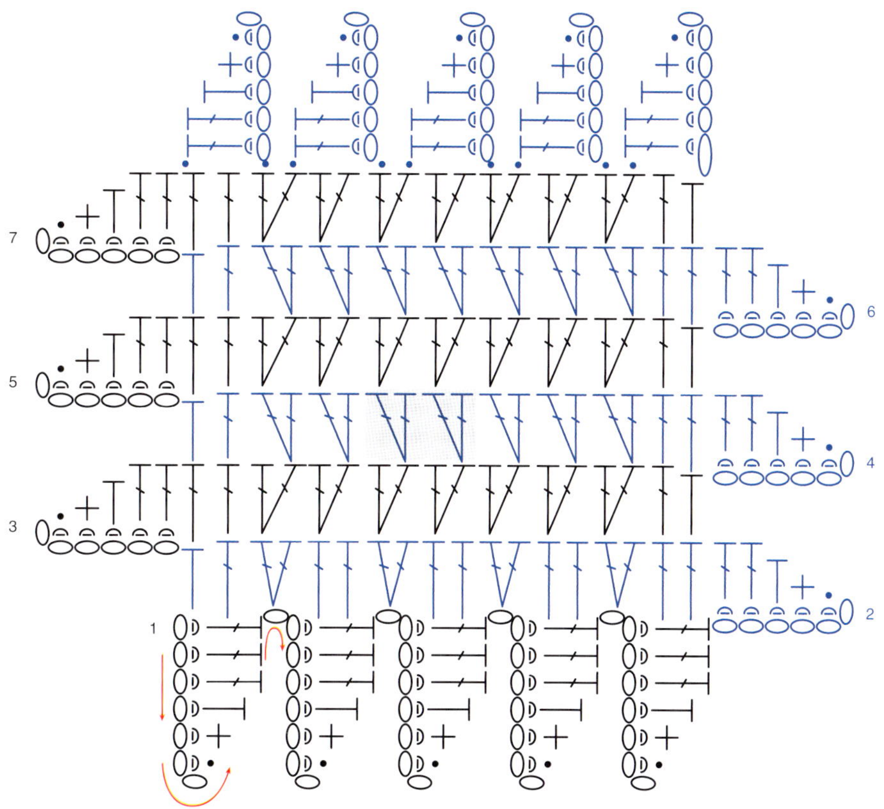

Banner Tabs
Stitch Diagram
Note: *Reps shown in gray.*

STITCH KEY

⬭	Chain (ch)
•	Slip stitch (sl st)
⌒	Work in back bump of chain and back loop
+	Single crochet (sc)
T	Half double crochet (hdc)
⊤	Double crochet (dc)

Zigzag Puffs

Skill Level

 INTERMEDIATE

Pattern Note

Foundation chain is a multiple of 6 stitches plus 3; body of stitch pattern between side borders is a multiple of 4 stitches.

Special Stitch

Puff: In indicated st or sp, [yo, pull up long lp] 4 times *(9 lps on hook)*, yo, draw through all lps on hook.

Zigzag Puffs

Ch a multiple of 6 sts + 3 *(see Pattern Note)*.

Row 1 (start bottom border): Puff *(see Special Stitch)* in 3rd ch from hook, [sk next 4 chs, puff in next ch, ch 4, puff in next ch] across, turn.

Row 2 (start side borders): Ch 3, puff in first puff (not in ch), ch 1, sk next ch-4 sp and Puff, [dc in sp between puff just sk and next puff, sk next puff, 3 dc in next ch-4 sp, sk next puff] across to last ch-4 sp, 2 dc in last ch-4 sp, dc between last 2 puffs, ch 2, puff in last puff, turn.

Row 3 (RS): Ch 3, puff in next puff, ch 1, sk next ch-2 sp, dc in each of next 3 dc, [ch 1, puff in next dc, ch 1, sk next dc, dc in each of next 2 dc] across, ending last rep with dc in each of last 3 dc, ch 2, sk next ch-1 sp, puff in next puff, turn.

Row 4: Ch 3, puff in next puff, ch 1, sk next ch-2 sp, dc in each of next 3 dc, [ch 1, sk next ch-1 sp, puff in next puff, ch 1, sk next ch-1 sp, dc in each of next 2 dc] across, ending last rep with dc in each of last 3 dc, ch 2, sk next ch sp, puff in next puff, turn.

Rep row 4 to desired length minus bottom border, ending with a RS row.

Top Border

Note: *See rows numbered in red on Stitch Diagram for Top Border rows.*

Row 1: Ch 3, puff in next puff, ch 1, sk next ch-2 sp, dc in each of next 3 dc, [sk next ch-1 sp, dc in next puff, dc in next ch-1 sp, dc in each of next 2 dc] across, ending last rep with dc in each of last 3 dc, ch 2, sk next ch sp, puff in next puff, turn.

Row 2: Ch 5, puff in next puff *(do not ch 1)*, sk next ch-2 sp and first dc, [puff in next dc, ch 4, puff in next dc, sk next 2 dc] across through puff in next-to-last dc, sk next dc and ch-1 sp, puff in last puff, ch 3, puff in next ch, ch 1 to secure. Fasten off. ●

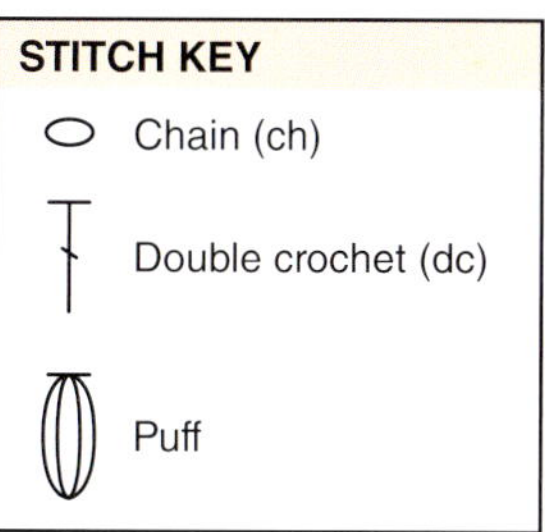

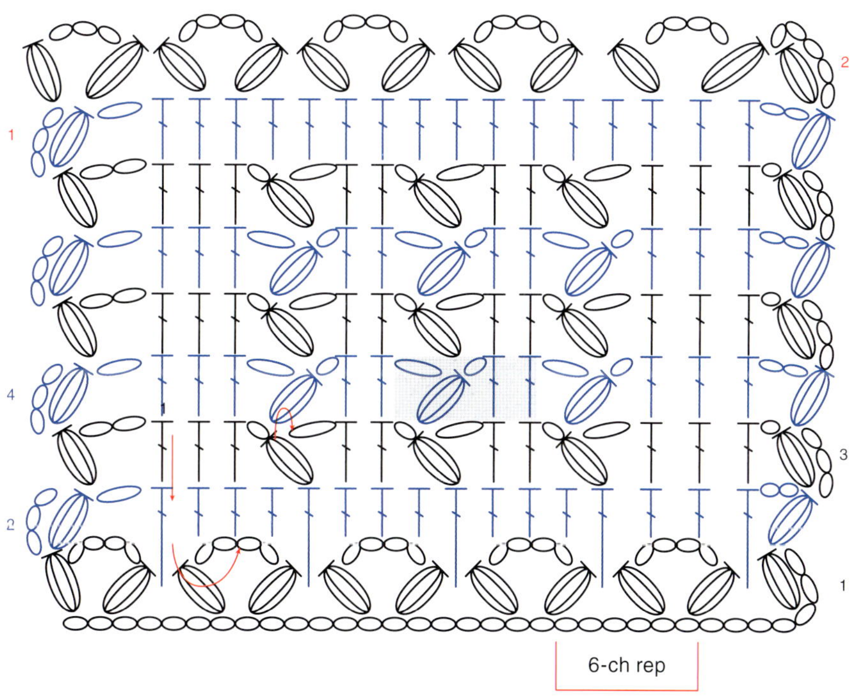

Zigzag Puffs
Stitch Diagram
Note: Reps shown in gray.

Tri-Leaves

Skill Level

■■■□ **INTERMEDIATE**

Pattern Notes

Stitch markers are needed for this stitch pattern.

Foundation chain is a multiple of 8 stitches plus 2; body of stitch pattern between side borders is a multiple of 8 stitches plus 7.

Turning chain at beginning of row counts as first stitch unless otherwise stated.

Chain-2 at beginning of even rows does not count as a stitch unless otherwise stated.

Special Stitches

Blade: Yo 3 times, insert hook in indicated st from back to front, yo, pull up lp, yo, draw through 2 lps, place marker around front strands of last 2 lps just worked, [yo, draw through 2 lps] twice, yo twice, insert hook under marked strands, yo, pull up lp, [yo, draw through 2 lps] twice. *(3 lps on hook, blade made)*

Right edge tri-leaf: Work **blade** *(see Special Stitches)* in base of st from row below to right of existing st, work blade in next sk st from row below *(5 lps on hook)*, sk first 4 dc on current row, work blade in next dc on current row *(7 lps on hook)*, yo, draw through all lps on hook.

Horizontal tri-leaf: Work blade in sk st from row below to the right of current st, work blade in next sk st in row below *(5 lps on hook)*, work blade in next sk st in row below to the left of current st *(7 lps on hook)*, yo, draw through all lps on hook.

Left edge tri-leaf: Work blade in last sk dc from current row, work blade in next sk st in row below *(5 lps on hook)*, work blade between last 2 sts in row below *(7 lps on hook)*, yo, draw through all lps on hook.

Leaflet: Working on RS, yo, insert hook from right to left around post of dc below last dc made, yo, pull up lp to height of current row, yo, draw through 2 lps on hook *(first leg made)*, sk next dc, insert hook from right to left around post of next dc, yo, pull up lp to height of current row, yo, draw through 2 lps on hook, yo, draw through all 3 lps on hook *(dc with last leg around it is next available st on current row)*.

Tri-Leaves

Ch a multiple of 8 sts + 2 *(see Pattern Notes)* loosely.

Row 1 (WS, start bottom border): Dc in 3rd ch from hook, dc in next ch, [sk next ch, 3 dc in next ch, sk next ch, dc in each of next 2 chs**, sk next ch, 2 dc in next ch, dc in next ch] across, ending last rep at **, dc in last ch, turn.

Row 2: Ch 2 *(see Pattern Notes)*, work **right edge tri-leaf** *(see Special Stitches)*, ch 1, dc in first and each of next 3 sk dc, sk next worked dc, 2 dc in next dc, dc in each of next 2 dc, [ch 1, work **horizontal tri-leaf** *(see Special Stitches)*, ch 2**, in current row, sk next dc, dc in each of next 7 dc] across, ending last rep at ** 9 sts from end, sk next dc, dc in each of next 2 dc, 2 dc in next dc, sk next dc, dc in each of next 2 dc, hdc in next dc, work **left edge tri-leaf** *(see Special Stitches)*, sk last st, turn.

Row 3: Ch 3, sk first tri-leaf st, dc in each of next 7 sts, [sk next 2 chs, hdc in next leaf st, sk next ch, dc in each of next 7 dc] across, ending last rep with dc in each of last 8 dc, sk remainder of row, turn.

Row 4: Ch 2, sk first st, dc in each st across to last st, hdc in last st, turn.

Row 5 (start side borders): Ch 3, sk first hdc, dc in each of next 2 sts, sk next dc, 2 dc in next dc, dc in each st across to last 5 sts, 2 dc in next dc, sk next dc, dc in each of last 3 sts, turn.

Row 6: Ch 2, work right edge tri-leaf, ch 1, in current row, dc in first and each of next 3 sk dc, sk next worked dc, 2 dc in next dc, dc in each of next 2 dc, [work **leaflet** *(see Special Stitches)*, dc in each of next 3 dc] across to last 5 sts, dc in same st just worked, sk 1 st, dc in each of next 2 sts, hdc in next st, work left edge tri-leaf, sk turning ch, turn.

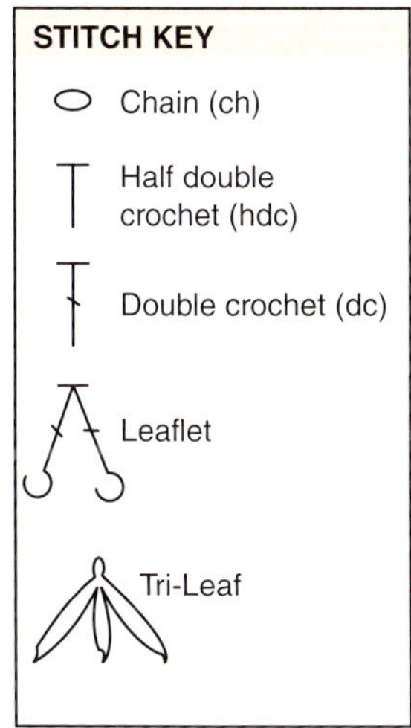

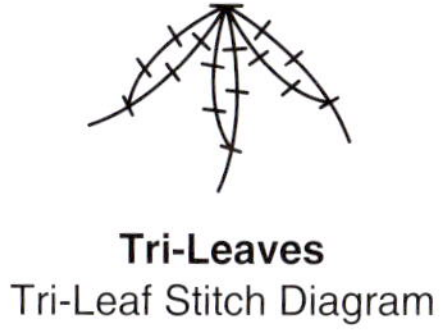

Tri-Leaves
Tri-Leaf Stitch Diagram

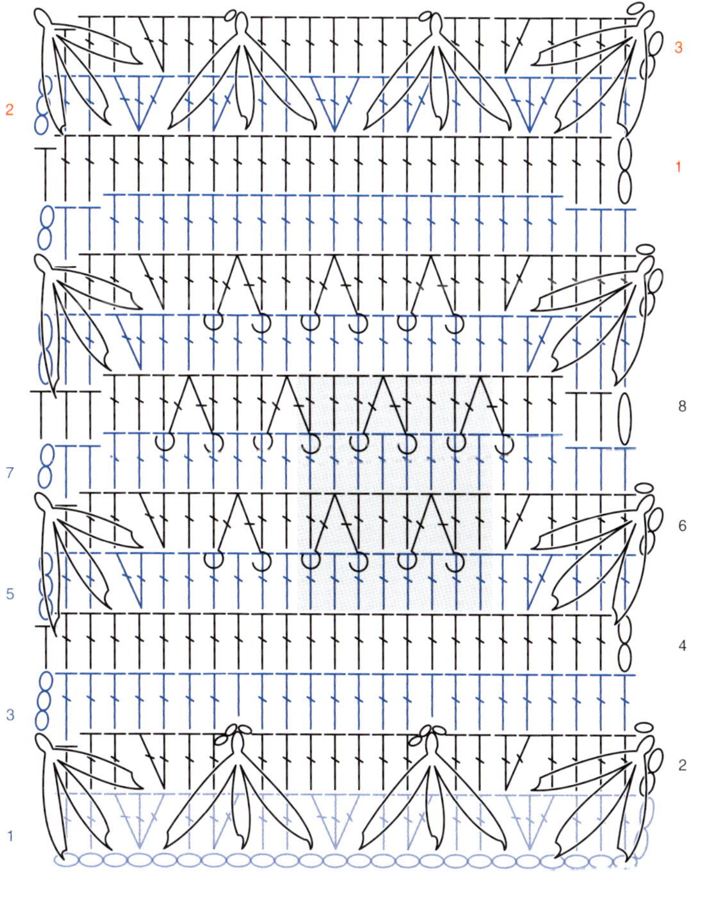

Tri-Leaves
Stitch Diagram
***Note:** Reps shown in gray.*

Row 7: Ch 2, sk first tri-leaf st, hdc in each of next 2 sts, dc in each st across to last 3 sts, hdc in each of next 3 dc, turn.

Row 8: Ch 1, sk first hdc, hdc in each of next 2 hdc, dc in each of next 3 dc, [work leaflet, dc in each of next 3 dc] across to last 3 sts, hdc in each of last 3 sts, turn.

[Rep rows 5–8] to desired length minus length of bottom border, ending with a row 7.

Top Border

Note: *See rows numbered in red on Stitch Diagram for Top Border rows.*

Row 1: Ch 3, sk first st, dc in each st across to last st, hdc in last st, turn.

Row 2: Ch 3, sk first hdc, dc in each of next 2 dc, [sk next dc, 3 dc in next dc, sk next dc, dc in each of next 2 dc**, sk next dc, 2 dc in next dc, dc in next dc] across, ending last rep at **, dc in last st, turn.

Row 3: Ch 2, work right edge tri-leaf, ch 1, working in sk sts on current row, dc in first and each of next 3 dc, sk next worked dc, dc in each of next 3 dc, [work horizontal tri-leaf, ch 1**, in current row, sk next dc, dc in each of next 7 dc] across, ending last rep at **, sk next dc, dc in each of next 3 dc, sk next dc, dc in each of next 2 dc, hdc in next dc, work left edge tri-leaf, sk turning ch, ch 1 to secure. Fasten off. ●

Wild Roses Ripple Lapghan

Skill Level

 INTERMEDIATE

Finished Sizes

Instructions given are for lapghan; changes for afghan are in [ ].

Finished Measurements

34 inches wide x 51 inches long [42½ inches wide x 63½ inches long]

Materials

- Plymouth Yarn Encore Worsted medium (worsted) weight acrylic/wool yarn (3½ oz/200 yds/100g per ball):
    3 [5] balls #0451 green gremlin
    3 [4] balls #1317 vacation blues
    3 [4] balls #0215 yellow
- Size I/9/5.5mm crochet hook or size needed to obtain gauge
- Tapestry needle

Gauge

12 dc = 4 inches; 12 dc rows = 8 inches

Pattern Notes

Weave in ends as work progresses.

Refer to Large Surface Flowers stitch pattern and diagrams on page 22.

It is helpful to make these flowers in the middle of some double crochet rows before attempting to work them in the foundation chain.

To change colors, work last yarn over and pull through with new color in last stitch of old color *(see Stitch Guide)*.

Chain-3 at beginning of row counts as first double crochet unless otherwise stated.

Special Stitches

Reverse slip stitch (rev sl st): Sl st from back to front in indicated lp or st.

Flower: Ch 5, 4 dc in 2 lps *(flower center)* of 4th ch from hook, *(first petal made)*, on WS, place marker in 2 strands at base of first dc made in first petal, **rev sl st** *(see Special Stitches)* in next st on current row, ch 1, fold main work away, (sl st, ch 2, 4 dc) in same 2 lps of flower center *(2nd petal made)*, remove hook from work and straighten so live st is now above last dc worked in current row, sl st in this dc, ch 1, [(sl st, ch 2, 4 dc, ch 2) in single strand rem in flower center] twice *(3rd and 4th petals made)*, rev sl st in marked strands on WS of first petal.

Flower back: On WS of flower, sl st loosely from right to left in 2 strands near top of 4th dc of 4th petal, sl st loosely in 2 strands near top of first dc of 3rd petal.

Lapghan

Row 1 (RS): With green, ch 102 [126] very loosely, dc in 4th ch from hook, [work **flower** *(see Special Stitches)*, 2 dc in next st, dc in each of next 3 sts, work flower, dc in each of next 3 sts, **dc dec** *(see Stitch Guide)* in next 2 sts, dc in next st, work flower, dc dec in next 2 sts, dc in each of next 4 sts, work flower, dc in each of next 2 sts, 2 dc in next st, dc in next st] across to 2 sts from end, work flower, dc in last st, **change to blue** *(see Pattern Notes and Stitch Guide)* and cut green, turn. *(17 [21] flowers)*

Row 2: Ch 3 *(see Pattern Notes)*, [work **flower back** *(see Special Stitches)*, 2 dc in next dc, dc in each of next 3 dc, work flower back, dc in each of next 2 dc, dc dec in next 2 dc, work flower back, dc dec in next 2 dc, dc in each of next 2 dc, work flower back, dc in each of next 3 dc, 2 dc in next dc] across to last flower, work flower back, dc in top of turning ch, turn.

Rows 3–6: Ch 3, dc in each of next 2 sts, [2 dc in next dc, dc in each of next 7 sts, dc dec in next 2 dc, dc in each of next 2 sts, dc dec in next 2 dc, dc in each of next 7 sts, 2 dc in next dc, dc in each of next 2 sts] across, ending last rep with dc in each of last 3 sts, turn. *(100 [124] dc)*

Row 7: Ch 3, dc in next dc, [work flower, 2 dc in next dc, dc in each of next 7 dc, dc dec in next 2 dc, dc in next dc, work flower, dc dec in next 2 dc, dc in each of next 7 dc, 2 dc in next dc, dc in next dc] across to last 2 dc, work flower, dc in top of turning ch, change to yellow, cut blue, turn.

Row 8: Ch 3, [work flower back, 2 dc in next dc, dc in each of next 7 dc, dc dec in next 2 dc, work flower back, dc dec in next 2 dc, dc in each of next 7 dc, 2 dc in next dc] across to last flower, work flower back, dc in top of turning ch, turn. *(9 [11] flowers)*

Rows 9–13: Rep rows 3–7.

Row 14: With green, rep row 8.

Rows 15–19: Rep rows 3–7.

Row 20: With blue, rep row 8.

[Rep rows 3–20] 2 [3] times.

[Rep rows 3–18] once.

Next row: Continuing with green, ch 3, dc in next dc, [work flower, 2 dc in next st, dc in each of next 3 sts, work flower, dc in each of next 3 sts, dc dec in next 2 sts, dc in next st, work flower, dc dec in next 2 sts, dc in each of next 4 sts, work flower, dc in each of next 2 sts, 2 dc in next st, dc in next st] across to 2 sts from end, work flower, dc in last st, turn. *(17 [21] flowers)*

Last row: Ch 1, [work flower back, 2 sc in next dc, sc in each of next 3 dc, work flower back, sc in each of next 2 dc, **sc dec** *(see Stitch Guide)* in next 2 dc, work flower back, sc dec in next 2 dc, sc in each of next 2 dc, work flower back, sc in next 3 dc, 2 sc in next dc] across to last flower, work flower back, sc in top of turning ch. Fasten off. ●

Readers Wrap

Skill Level

 INTERMEDIATE

Finished Measurements

16 inches wide x 58 inches long

Materials
- Plymouth Yarn Encore Worsted medium (worsted) weight acrylic/wool yarn (3½ oz/200 yds/100g per ball):

  3 balls #1204 brownstone

  2 balls #6001 raccoon

  2 balls #0240 taupe

  1 ball #0146 winter white
- Size I/9/5.5mm crochet hook or size needed to obtain gauge
- 70 stitch markers
- Tapestry needle

Gauge

12 dc = 4 inches; 12 dc rows = 6½ inches

Pattern Notes

Weave in ends as work progresses.

Refer to Twisted Loops stitch pattern and diagram on page 9.

Chain-3 at beginning of row counts as first double crochet unless otherwise stated.

To change colors, work last yarn over and pull through with new color in last stitch of old color.

Rows with side borders contain extra short-row turns.

Special Stitches

Reverse slip stitch (rev sl st): Sl st from back to front in indicated lp or st.

Twisted loop: Ch 5, with yarn held to right of hook, **rev sl st** *(see Special Stitches)* in 1 designated lp only of indicated st. Keep all twisted loops on RS of work.

Right-side double crochet—single crochet—(RS dc—RS sc): When working into a st from the RS that already has a twisted lp worked into either the front or back lp, insert the hook under both lps to the left of the sl st, but in the same st.

Wrap

Row 1 (WS): With brownstone, ch 188 loosely, working loosely in back lps only, sc in 2nd ch from hook and in each ch across, turn. *(187 sts)*

Row 2: Sl st in both lps of first st, mark front lp of st just made, [sk next 2 sts, work **twisted loop** *(see Special Stitches)* in front lp of next st] across, mark back lp of last sl st made, turn.

Row 3: Working in front of twisted loops in same row as sl sts just made, sk first worked st and next unworked st, [work twisted loop in back lp of next unworked st, sk next worked and next unworked st] across, ending after last rep with twisted loop in last unworked st, sl st normally in marked lp of last sl st, remove marker, turn.

Row 4 (RS): Ch 3 *(see Pattern Notes)*, working in same row as twisted loops, sk first st and the sl st in it, work **RS dc** *(see Special Stitches)* in next st, [dc in next unworked st, work RS dc in next 2 sts] across to last 2 sts, dc in next unworked st, sk last worked st of same row, dc in marked lp of next sl st, remove marker, turn, **change to raccoon** *(see Pattern Notes and Stitch Guide)*.

Row 5: With raccoon, ch 3, dc in each dc across, turn.

Rows 6–8: Rep rows 2–4.

Row 9: With brownstone, ch 3, sk first dc, dc in each dc across, turn.

Rows 10–12: Rep rows 2–4.

Row 13: With taupe, rep row 9.

Row 14 (start side borders):

A. Sl st in both lps of first st, mark front lp of sl st just made, [sk next 2 sts, work twisted loop in front lp of next st] 3 times, mark back lp of last sl st made, **turn** *(see Pattern Notes)*;

B. working with twisted loops folded away and in same row as sl sts just made, sk first occupied st and next unworked st, [work twisted loop in back lp of next unworked st, sk next occupied and next unworked st] twice, work twisted loop in last unworked st, sl st normally in marked lp of last sl st, turn;

C. ch 3, sk first dc and the sl st in it, work RS dc in next dc, [dc in next unworked dc, work RS dc in next 2 dc] twice, dc in next unworked dc, sk next occupied dc, sc in marked lp of next sl st, dc in next and each dc across to last 10 dc;

D. ch 3, sl st in next dc, mark front lp of sl st just made, [sk next 2 sts, work twisted loop in front lp of next st] 3 times, mark back lp of last sl st made, turn;

E. working with twisted loops folded away and in same row as sl sts just made, [sk next occupied st and next unworked st, work twisted loop in back lp of next unworked st] twice, sk next occupied and next unworked st, ch 5, sl st normally in marked lp of last sl st, turn;

F. ch 2, sk first dc and the sl st in it, dc in next st, [dc in next unworked dc, work RS dc in next 2 dc] twice, dc in last unworked dc, dc in marked lp of next sl st, remove all markers, turn.

Row 15 (WS): With white, ch 3, dc in next 7 dc, yo, insert hook in next dc, sk ch-2, insert hook from front to back in top of ch-3, yo, pull up lp, [yo, draw through 2 lps] twice, dc in same ch-3, dc in next and each st across, turn.

Row 16: Rep row 14.

Rows 17–30: [Rep rows 15 and 16 alternately] 7 times, changing colors every 2 rows in the following sequence: taupe, brownstone, raccoon, brownstone, taupe, white, taupe.

Row 31: With brownstone, rep row 15.

Rows 32–34: Rep rows 2–4.

Row 35: With raccoon, rep row 5.

Rows 36–38: Rep rows 2–4.

Rows 39–41: With brownstone, rep rows 35–37.

Row 42: Ch 1, working in same row as twisted loops, sk first st and the sl st in it, work sc in next st, [sc in next unworked st, work **RS sc** *(see Special Stitches)* in each of next 2 sts] across to last 2 sts, sc in next unworked st, sk last worked st of same row, sl st in back lp of marked sl st, remove marker. Fasten off.

Pocket
Make 2.

Rows 1–4: With white, ch 26 loosely, rep rows 1–4 of main pattern.

Rows 5–24: [Rep rows 5–8 of Wrap] 5 times, changing colors every 4 rows in the following sequence: taupe, brownstone, raccoon, brownstone, taupe.

Rows 25–27: With white, rep rows 5–7 of Wrap.

Row 28: Rep row 42 of Wrap. Fasten off.

Assembly
Position first Pocket approximately 4 inches from 1 end of Wrap, matching color stripes. Sew onto Wrap around sides and bottom with opening facing main part of Wrap. Rep for 2nd Pocket on other end of Wrap. ●

Baby Cap & Blanket

Skill Level

INTERMEDIATE

Finished Measurements

Cap: 6½ inches high x 13 inches in circumference

Blanket: 30 inches wide x 35 inches long

Materials

- Plymouth Yarn Dreambaby DK light (DK) weight acrylic/nylon yarn (1¾ oz/183 yds/50g per ball): 4 balls each #0101 winter white and #0143 lima bean (for blanket and cap)
- Size G/6/4mm crochet hook or size needed to obtain gauge
- Tapestry needle

Gauge

16 dc = 4 inches; 7 dc rows = 4 inches

Pattern Notes

Weave in ends as work progresses.

Refer to Tri-Leaves stitch pattern and diagram on page 54.

For cap, work foundation row and first row in white. Then alternate colors every 2 rows, ending with last single row in green. Cut yarn after every color change.

Special Stitches

First foundation single crochet (first foundation sc): Ch 2, insert hook into 2nd ch from hook, yo, pull up lp, yo, pull through 1 lp on hook *(ch-1 completed)*, yo, pull through all lps on hook *(sc completed)*.

Next foundation single crochet (next foundation sc): [Insert hook in last ch-1 made, yo, pull up lp, yo, pull through 1 lp on hook *(ch-1 made)*, yo, pull through all lps on hook *(sc made)*] as indicated.

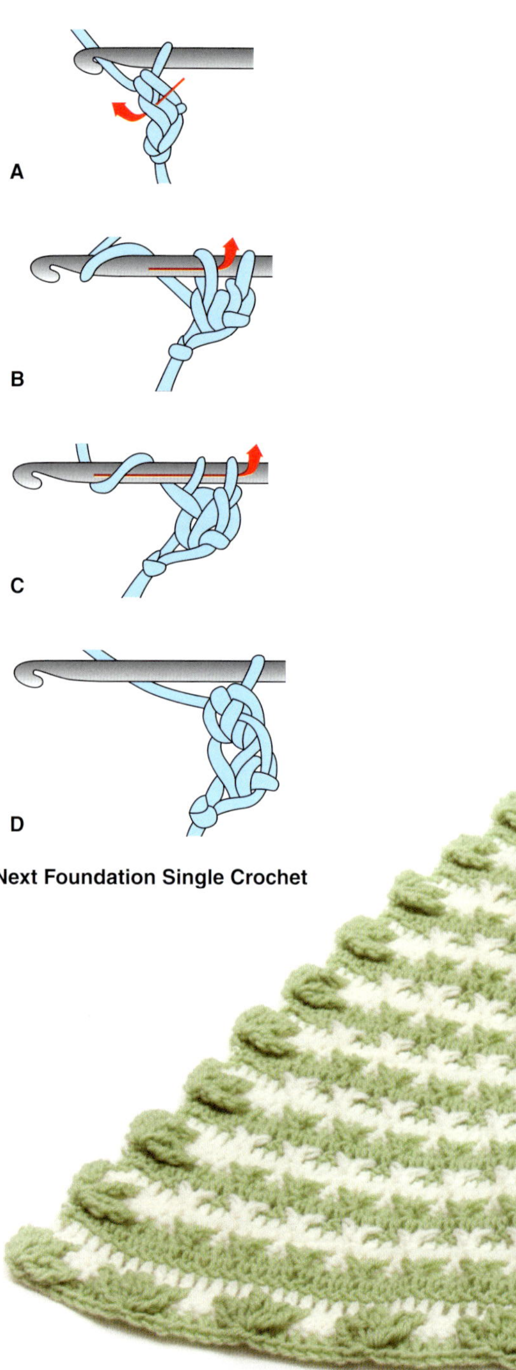

Next Foundation Single Crochet

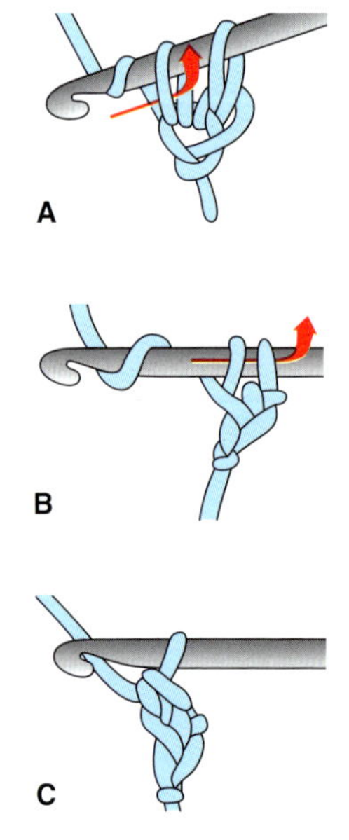

First Foundation Single Crochet

Baby Cap

Cap Panel

Make 2.

Row 1: Work **first foundation sc** *(see Special Stitches)*, work 23 **next foundation sc** *(see Special Stitches)*. *(24 sts)*

Row 2: Ch 2, dc in each of next 2 sts, [sk next st, 3 dc in next st, sk next st, dc in each of next 2 sts**, sk next st, 2 dc in next st, dc in next st] across, ending last rep at **, dc in last st, turn.

Rows 3–9: Work rows 2–8 of Tri-Leaves pattern alternating colors every 2 rows *(see Pattern Notes)*.

Rows 10–12: Continuing in established stripe sequence, work Top Border rows 1–3 of Tri-Leaves pattern.

Finishing

Sew panels tog along top and sides, leaving stretchy foundation row to fit around head.

Baby Blanket

Ch 114 loosely.

Rows 1–78: [Rep rows 1–8 of Tri-Leaves st pattern consecutively] 10 times, ending with row 7.

Rows 79–81: Work last 3 rows of st pattern.

Fasten off. ●

Headband

Skill Level

■■□□ EASY

Finished Measurements

1¼ inches wide x
19½ inches long

Materials

- Plymouth Yarn Encore Tweed medium (worsted) weight acrylic/wool/rayon yarn (3½ oz/200 yds/100g per ball):
    1 ball #T100 nugget
- Size I/9/5.5mm crochet hook or size needed to obtain gauge
- Tapestry needle
- 2 size 1/0 or similar snaps
- Sewing needle and thread

Gauge

4 dc = 1¼ inches; 2 dc rows = 1¼ inches

Pattern Notes

Weave in ends as work progresses.

Refer to Zigzag Chain Braids border pattern and diagrams on page 13.

Chain-3 at beginning of row counts as first double crochet unless otherwise stated.

Special Stitches

Plait: Ch 13, sl st in 2 lps of 13th ch from hook. Keep plaits on RS.

Fastening Stitch (FS): Insert hook in last plait pulled up, yo, pull lp through plait only, yo, insert hook in designated dc, yo, pull up lp, yo, draw through 2 lps on hook, yo, draw through all 3 lps on hook.

Headband

Row 1: Ch 5, sc in 2nd ch from hook and in next ch, sl st in next ch, work **plait** *(see Special Stitches)*, mark as beg plait, sl st in last ch, turn.

Row 2 (RS): Ch 3 *(see Pattern Notes)*, working behind plait, sk first 2 sl sts, 2 dc in next sc, work plait, mark as 2nd plait, dc in last sc, turn.

Row 3: Ch 3, sk first dc, skipping and keeping plait on RS, dc in each of next 2 dc, work plait, dc in last st, turn.

Rep row 3 to 1¼ inches less than desired length.

Next row: Ch 3, sk first dc, skipping plaits, dc in each of next 3 sts, turn.

Next row: Ch 2, working on RS, braid border plaits tog as follows: Taking care not to twist plaits, working from bottom, pull marked 2nd plait through marked beg plait, zigzagging plaits, continue to pull each plait through the plait above it, work **FS** *(see Special Stitches)* in first dc, dc in each of next 3 dc, turn.

Last row: Ch 1, sk first st, sc in each of next 3 sts, sl st in top of turning ch. Fasten off.

Finishing

Sew 2 snaps to ends with sockets on WS of row 1 made and studs on RS at base of last sc row made. ●

STITCH GUIDE

Need help? ▶ **StitchGuide.com** • ILLUSTRATED GUIDES • HOW-TO VIDEOS

STITCH ABBREVIATIONS

beg	begin/begins/beginning
bpdc	back post double crochet
bpsc	back post single crochet
bptr	back post treble crochet
CC	contrasting color
ch(s)	chain(s)
ch-	refers to chain or space previously made (i.e., ch-1 space)
ch sp(s)	chain space(s)
cl(s)	cluster(s)
cm	centimeter(s)
dc	double crochet (singular/plural)
dc dec	double crochet 2 or more stitches together, as indicated
dec	decrease/decreases/decreasing
dtr	double treble crochet
ext	extended
fpdc	front post double crochet
fpsc	front post single crochet
fptr	front post treble crochet
g	gram(s)
hdc	half double crochet
hdc dec	half double crochet 2 or more stitches together, as indicated
inc	increase/increases/increasing
lp(s)	loop(s)
MC	main color
mm	millimeter(s)
oz	ounce(s)
pc	popcorn(s)
rem	remain/remains/remaining
rep(s)	repeat(s)
rnd(s)	round(s)
RS	right side
sc	single crochet (singular/plural)
sc dec	single crochet 2 or more stitches together, as indicated
sk	skip/skipped/skipping
sl st(s)	slip stitch(es)
sp(s)	space(s)/spaced
st(s)	stitch(es)
tog	together
tr	treble crochet
trtr	triple treble
WS	wrong side
yd(s)	yard(s)
yo	yarn over

YARN CONVERSION

OUNCES TO GRAMS		GRAMS TO OUNCES	
1	28.4	25	7/8
2	56.7	40	1 2/3
3	85.0	50	1 3/4
4	113.4	100	3 1/2

UNITED STATES		UNITED KINGDOM
sl st (slip stitch)	=	sc (single crochet)
sc (single crochet)	=	dc (double crochet)
hdc (half double crochet)	=	htr (half treble crochet)
dc (double crochet)	=	tr (treble crochet)
tr (treble crochet)	=	dtr (double treble crochet)
dtr (double treble crochet)	=	ttr (triple treble crochet)
skip	=	miss

Reverse single crochet (reverse sc): Ch 1, sk first st, working from left to right, insert hook in next st from front to back, draw up lp on hook, yo and draw through both lps on hook.

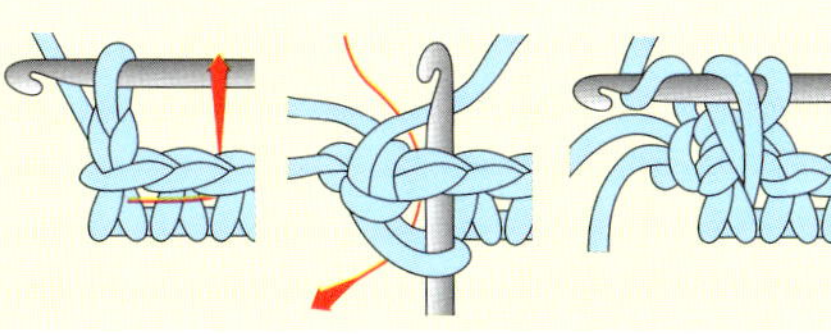

Chain (ch): Yo, pull through lp on hook.

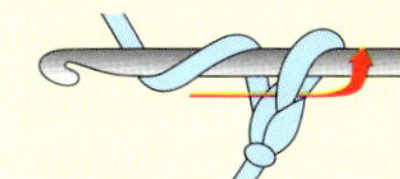

Single crochet (sc): Insert hook in st, yo, pull through st, yo, pull through both lps on hook.

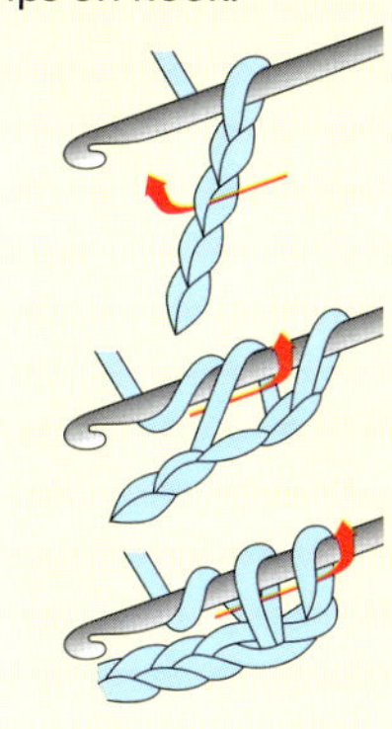

Double crochet (dc): Yo, insert hook in st, yo, pull through st, [yo, pull through 2 lps] twice.

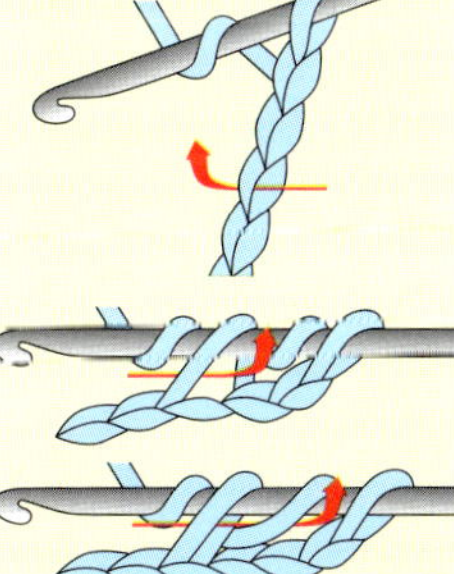
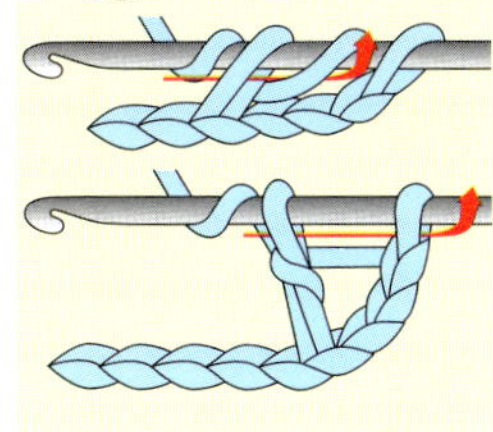

Front loop (front lp) Back loop (back lp)

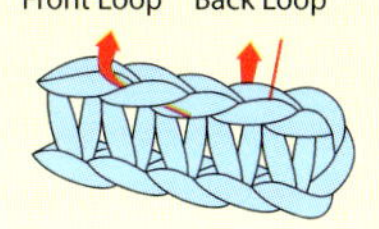

Front post stitch (fp): Back post stitch (bp): When working post st, insert hook from right to left around post of st on previous row.

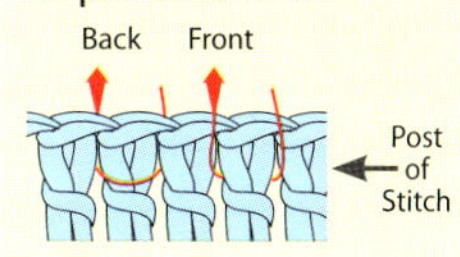

Half double crochet (hdc): Yo, insert hook in st, yo, pull through st, yo, pull through all 3 lps on hook.

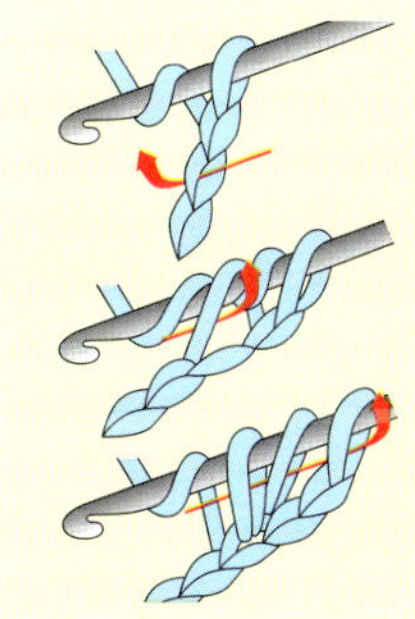

Double treble crochet (dtr): Yo 3 times, insert hook in st, yo, pull through st, [yo, pull through 2 lps] 4 times.

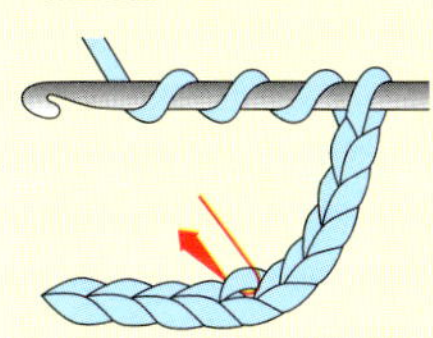

Slip stitch (sl st): Insert hook in st, pull through both lps on hook.

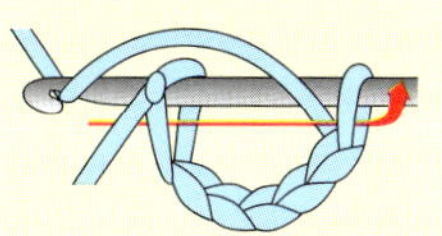

Chain color change (ch color change) Yo with new color, draw through last lp on hook.

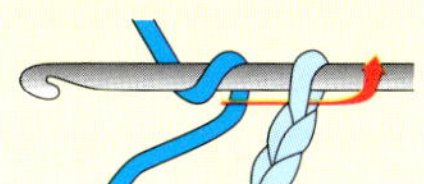

Double crochet color change (dc color change) Drop first color, yo with new color, draw through last 2 lps of st.

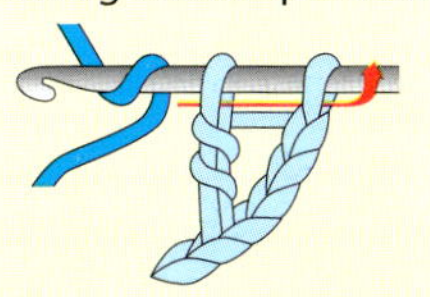

Treble crochet (tr): Yo twice, insert hook in st, yo, pull through st, [yo, pull through 2 lps] 3 times.

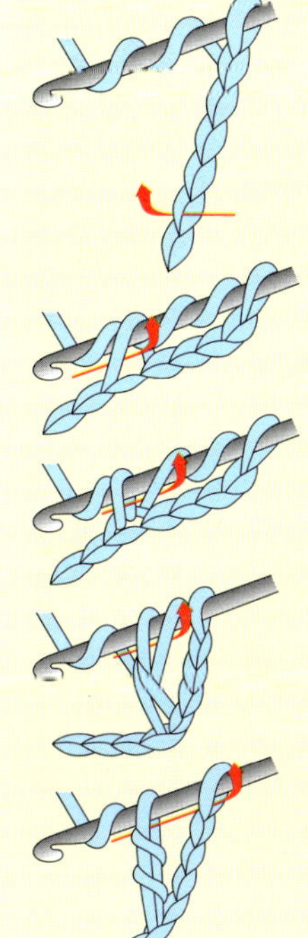

Single crochet decrease (sc dec): (Insert hook, yo, draw lp through) in each of the sts indicated, yo, draw through all lps on hook.

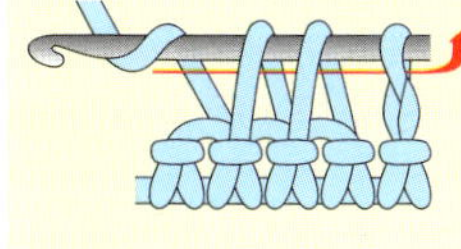

Example of 2-sc dec

Half double crochet decrease (hdc dec): (Yo, insert hook, yo, draw lp through) in each of the sts indicated, yo, draw through all lps on hook.

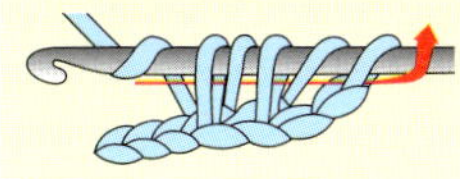

Example of 2-hdc dec

Double crochet decrease (dc dec): (Yo, insert hook, yo, draw lp through, yo, draw through 2 lps on hook) in each of the sts indicated, yo, draw through all lps on hook.

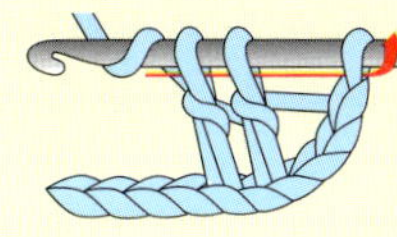

Example of 2-dc dec

Treble crochet decrease (tr dec): Holding back last lp of each st, tr in each of the sts indicated, yo, pull through all lps on hook.

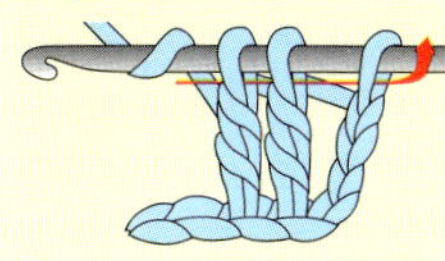

Example of 2-tr dec

Metric Conversion Charts

<table>
<tr><td colspan="4">METRIC CONVERSIONS</td></tr>
<tr><td>yards</td><td>x</td><td>.9144</td><td>=</td><td>metres (m)</td></tr>
<tr><td>yards</td><td>x</td><td>91.44</td><td>=</td><td>centimetres (cm)</td></tr>
<tr><td>inches</td><td>x</td><td>2.54</td><td>=</td><td>centimetres (cm)</td></tr>
<tr><td>inches</td><td>x</td><td>25.40</td><td>=</td><td>millimetres (mm)</td></tr>
<tr><td>inches</td><td>x</td><td>.0254</td><td>=</td><td>metres (m)</td></tr>
</table>

centimetres	x	.3937	=	inches
metres	x	1.0936	=	yards

INCHES INTO MILLIMETRES & CENTIMETRES (Rounded off slightly)

inches	mm	cm	inches	cm	inches	cm	inches	cm
1/8	3	0.3	5	12.5	21	53.5	38	96.5
1/4	6	0.6	5 1/2	14	22	56	39	99
3/8	10	1	6	15	23	58.5	40	101.5
1/2	13	1.3	7	18	24	61	41	104
5/8	15	1.5	8	20.5	25	63.5	42	106.5
3/4	20	2	9	23	26	66	43	109
7/8	22	2.2	10	25.5	27	68.5	44	112
1	25	2.5	11	28	28	71	45	114.5
1 1/4	32	3.2	12	30.5	29	73.5	46	117
1 1/2	38	3.8	13	33	30	76	47	119.5
1 3/4	45	4.5	14	35.5	31	79	48	122
2	50	5	15	38	32	81.5	49	124.5
2 1/2	65	6.5	16	40.5	33	84	50	127
3	75	7.5	17	43	34	86.5		
3 1/2	90	9	18	46	35	89		
4	100	10	19	48.5	36	91.5		
4 1/2	115	11.5	20	51	37	94		

KNITTING NEEDLES CONVERSION CHART

Canada/U.S.	0	1	2	3	4	5	6	7	8	9	10	10½	11	13	15
Metric (mm)	2	2¼	2¾	3¼	3½	3¾	4	4½	5	5½	6	6½	8	9	10

CROCHET HOOKS CONVERSION CHART

Canada/U.S.	1/B	2/C	3/D	4/E	5/F	6/G	8/H	9/I	10/J	10½/K	N
Metric (mm)	2.25	2.75	3.25	3.5	3.75	4.25	5	5.5	6	6.5	9.0

Annie's®

Built-In Crochet Borders is published by Annie's, 306 East Parr Road, Berne, IN 46711. Printed in USA. Copyright © 2014 Annie's. All rights reserved. This publication may not be reproduced in part or in whole without written permission from the publisher.

RETAIL STORES: If you would like to carry this publication or any other Annie's publication, visit AnniesWSL.com.

Every effort has been made to ensure that the instructions in this publication are complete and accurate. We cannot, however, take responsibility for human error, typographical mistakes or variations in individual work. Please visit AnniesCustomerService.com to check for pattern updates.

ISBN: 978-1-57367-595-6

1 2 3 4 5 6 7 8 9